THE
APHRODISIAC
P⟨OF⟩WER

by

Sir Oliver Popplewell

**Grosvenor House
Publishing Limited**

This book is published by
Grosvenor House Publishing Ltd
28-30 High Street, Guildford, Surrey, GU1 3EL.
www.grosvenorhousepublishing.co.uk

A CIP record for this book
is available from the British Library

ISBN 978-1-78623-021-8

Dedication

(For Liz)

CONTENTS

CHAPTER ONE

THE APHRODISIAC OF POWER

Politicians are not the only ones to commit adultery, but they are the ones which tend to attract public opprobrium and cause public scandal. Kings and presidents do the same. Their behaviour, like that of other people, has not changed over the decades. A.J.P.Taylor suggests that Gladstone had identified six previous Prime Ministers in the 19th century, who had been adulterers. Sexual appetites grow no less as the years go by and politicians still feel able to indulge in such activities, in the confident belief that they will not be discovered. In an age of instant communication and intrusive media interest, it is unlikely now, certainly in Britain where there are effectively no laws of privacy, that the love affairs of Asquith or Lloyd George, distinguished politicians and wartime Prime Ministers, would remain hidden from the general public for some fifty years. But it is not only politicians, or kings or presidents who want to exercise their power. Newspaper proprietors operate in a different field and use their power for a rather different reason. They not only want to increase the sales of their publications but they also want to use that power, both to make policy, and to influence events.

What then is the driving force that causes them all to behave in this way? Mathew Parris, the well-known politician and now a much respected political commentator, describes it as the "Aphrodisiac of Power". He analysed the pathology of the politician in this way—"elective office feeds your vanity and starves your self-respect. What then are the compensations that, for those who choose this life, make it worthwhile? First a craving for applause, for being a somebody, for being looked up to.

The re-read across from this to the sexual behaviour of middle-aged men in politics is too obvious to need stating; power is, indeed, an aphrodisiac; but for the powerful, for the predator rather than his prey, it is like having a big sports car".

"Secondly, a completely and persistently unrealistic belief in your own good luck. Third, and this is truly weird, an awfully thin skin; all this leads to frequent pain, frequent euphoria, an obsessive drive to keep asking for more until something big and external to yourself finally fells you."[1] For the prey, too, there is the excitement of engaging in an illicit affair, in sharing state secrets, and in being consulted about important decisions. There is also, not to be underestimated, the enormous prestige and perhaps glamour, inherent in a relationship with a man of power. Thus for the predator and prey alike, an affair has enormous attraction. In June 1885, Sir Charles Dilke, a possible future Liberal Prime Minister wrote to Mrs Pattison, his mistress, "It is in old age that power comes. It is possible for an old man in English politics to exert enormous power without effort, and with but little call upon his time, and no drain at all upon his health and vital force. It is in old age that power comes, that can be used legitimately by the once strong man."[2]

David Owen, the well-known politician, who was Foreign Secretary wrote a book *The Hubris Syndrome*, in which he described the intoxication of power. He was particularly referring to the part played by George Bush and Tony Blair in going to war in Iraq. But "intoxication of power" has a wider context and while it necessarily covers the attitude of politicians it is by no means, as we shall, see, confined to them. And, as we shall also see, while the power is often exercised in a sexual context, it has very many other objects. "Hubris", says Owen "is almost an occupational hazard for leading politicians as it is for leaders in other fields—for it feeds on the isolation which often builds up around such leaders."[3] Owen sets out just some of symptoms

---

1 *The Spectator*, 21 May 2011
2 Dilke Papers, 21 May 2011 British Museum. D.P.43906, 106
3 Owen, David *The Hubris Syndrome* (Methuen & Co, London 2012) p xvi

which may trigger a diagnosis of hubris. They include "a predisposition to take actions to cast themselves in a good light, a disproportionate concern with image, excessive confidence in their own judgements and exaggerated self- belief, bordering on a sense of omnipotence.[4] Bertrand Russell (the philosopher) described how "when the check on pride is removed, a certain kind of madness occurs, namely the intoxication of power."[5]

On another occasion Parris wrote: "Why do M.Ps and VIPs – and public figures take such risks. What Oscar Wilde called "feasting with panthers" is an apt expression for every sort of adventure. It means hazard. It means foolish, reckless excitement. It means danger, secrecy and shame."[6] Secrecy and danger are the reason for the folly. They are the spice and the drug. He observes that people in public life, who are self-selected, are drawn into a political career which, once secured, turns previously cautious people into secret risk takers. "They are united by a craving for applause—it offers publicity—you *are* somebody."[7]

4 Ibid pp 1 and 2
5 Russell, Bertrand. *A History of Western Philosophy* (Allen and Unwin. London 2nd edition 1961) p 782
6 Parris, Matthew. *Great Parliamentary Scandals* (Robson Books. Ltd. London.1995) p xiii
7 Ibid pp xiv-xv

CHAPTER TWO

DISRAELI, HIS LOVES
AND THE QUEEN

Disraeli was born in 1804. He had a distinguished political career which lasted for most of the 19th century and was a worthy rival to his Liberal opponent, Gladstone. He created the modern Conservative party and was Prime Minister twice. He was not only a highly astute politician, and one of the great statesmen of his time, but he was also the author of a number of highly acclaimed political novels which are still read today.

Because his father could not afford to give him a proper private or University education, Disraeli was forced to be trained as a solicitor, but his literary interests were in the classics and not in law books. His interest in politics, however, resulted in his being elected MP for Maidstone (his fifth attempt at a seat) in 1837. His attempts to enter the business world by investing in speculative joint stock companies ended in disaster, as did an attempt to start a Conservative newspaper. He was left in considerable debt and he spent much of his time trying to escape the clutches of his creditors. His parents and, in particular, his dominating sister Sarah, were very anxious to see him married if only to ensure that he settled down and had access to money. A whole bevy of attractive ladies now appeared in Disraeli's life.

The first was Clara Bolton, who became his mistress in 1832. She was married to a doctor who seems to have been indifferent to the situation. The relationship lasted for no more than a year. She was described as vulgar and somewhat brassy.[8] Others thought

---

8 Blake, Robert. *Disraeli* (Eyre and Spottiswoode. London. 1966) p 76

that she was socially pretentious, conceited, devious and unprincipled.[9] Eventually she returned to her husband and then left him to become the mistress of Sir Francis Sykes, the husband of Henrietta Sykes, who now, in turn, became Disraeli's mistress. In between these various arrangements, Disraeli had proposed to Ellen Meredith and been rejected. He fell in love with Helen Blackwood, one of the beautiful granddaughters of the playwright Sheridan. She was the wife of a naval officer, who was often abroad, but it was another love affair that ended his romance with Helen. "She had been his chief admiration, more beautiful than her beautiful sisters. Dreams! dreams! dreams!"[10] Lady Charlotte Bertie was another of Disraeli's lovers. They met at the opera and he confided in Sarah "How would you like Lady Z (Charlotte Bertie) for a sister in law, very clever, £25,000 and domestic".[11] In fact she had little money and was determined to escape an unhappy family by seeking security. She therefore decided to marry the rich MP, Sir John Guest, who owned an ironworks.

But it was Henrietta Sykes who for three years dominated Disraeli's love life. He first met her in the spring of 1834. Her husband, Sir Francis, had poor health and liked to get out of England either on the Continent or on his yacht. She was variously described as" a sensuous beauty, with dark hair, large eyes, pouting lips, well rounded shoulders and bosom,"[12] "basically a passionate, emotional, jealous, highly sexed woman who wanted a lover."[13] All was not peaceful, however, because Sir Francis threatened to make the liaison public. Henrietta retaliated by calling at Sarah Bolton's house (previously Disraeli's, but now Sir Francis', mistress) and found them both "intimate". Sarah continued to harass Disraeli, but Sir Francis was persuaded not to interfere. In April 1834 he went on a prolonged tour of Europe, not returning until late in 1836. She and Disraeli lived openly in the Sykes' house in London.

---

9 Hibbert, Christopher. *Disraeli*. (Harper Collins. London.2004.) p80
10 Ibid p 61
11 *Correspondence with his Sister*, p 20
12 Bradford, Sarah. *Disraeli*. (Weidenfeld and Nicolson Ltd, London 1982) p 64.
13 Blake p 100

However there were further problems when Henrietta also became the mistress of Lord Lyndhurst, who was now one of Disraeli's mentors. He was a well-known womaniser and a former Conservative Lord Chancellor, who could exercise considerable patronage. She undoubtedly helped Disraeli by her liaison in advancing his political career, but the scandal damaged his reputation for years to come. By the autumn of 1836 the affair had come to an end. It is not clear whether he had tired of her incessant motherly devotion and possessiveness or whether her affair with the artist, David Maclise, caused it. He scarcely ever saw her again although he kept all her love letters. She died in May 1846 ostracised by society.

In April 1832, he had first met Mary Anne Lewis, the wife of a fellow candidate of his at Maidstone, Wyndham Lewis. Disraeli described her as "a pretty little woman, a flirt and a rattle, and gifted with a volubility I should think unequalled."[14] She had been born in 1792 and married Wyndham in 1815. He died in 1838. Before that she had had a friendship with Disraeli, which, after Wyndham's death, grew stronger. That Disraeli was motivated in his pursuit of her by the belief that she was rich is borne out in his correspondence, but it is equally clear that, when he discovered that she was not wealthy, he was nonetheless determined to marry her for love, which he did in August 1839. When she died in 1872 he expressed the view that "Marriage is the greatest earthly happiness when founded on complete sympathy."[15]

Mary Anne was in fact a person of a jealous and possessive nature with some mental instability, who made incessant demands on Disraeli. She violently objected to his writing privately to his sister Sarah and to Sarah sending letters to him without her knowledge. This was a constant source of friction, with intermittent passages of crisis and reconciliation, between the three. One letter written in 1849 by Disraeli to Sarah gives some insight into their relationship, as well as reference to a clandestine love affair:

---

14 *Correspondence* p 6.
15 Bradford p 300

"The storm which was more or less been brewing in my sky for the last 12 months burst rather suddenly yesterday—an access of jealousy brought affairs to a crisis & I found all my private locks forced and instead of love letters there were only lawyers bills and pecuniary documents—it is the necessary consequence of her violent temper and scenes".

He then makes reference to an alibi given by Sarah when he had told Mary Anne that he was going to Bucks Assizes, which Mary Anne had learnt was untrue. He was probably having an affair with Lady Londonderry.[16] He was always having problems with his debts which he was anxious to conceal from Mary Anne. But, notwithstanding her temperament, the marriage settled down into a very happy relationship with no further indication of marital infidelity.

After she died in 1872, the next woman in Disraeli's life was the Dowager Countess of Cardigan. She had been Cardigan's mistress before becoming his second wife. She was rich, wanted power and throughout 1873 pursued Disraeli. She offered to act as his private secretary and political hostess but wanted marriage. When she proposed, Disraeli turned her down. The predator had suddenly become the prey. In June 1873, she wrote: "I have had 12 offers of marriage since Lord Cardigan's death but have long decided upon the union which would to me secure happiness, comfort and the realisation of my most ambitious hopes." She went on to describe the proposed alliance as "of the greatest man we have in genius and intellect with the wealthiest relict of the staunchest Peer that ever lived."[17] She subsequently married the Comte de Lancastre and lived until 1916.

In 1873, Disraeli first met Selina, Countess of Bradford, and, within months, was writing to her with great passion, sometimes twice a day, and calling on her whenever he could. Over 1000 of his letters were found at her family seat. He sought her advice on the award of honours and posts. He was now 68 and she was a

16 *Correspondence.* vol v p 197.
17 Blake p 530

married woman of 54 years. Their relationship was often tempestuous and it seems likely that, while he found it cathartic to unburden himself of his innermost thoughts, she seems not to have reciprocated his amorous advances, In 1874, he had written: "When you have the government of a country on your shoulders to *love* a person and to be *in love* with a person makes all the difference—the difficulty of seeing your beloved or communicating with her, only animates and excites you, I have devised schemes of seeing, or writing to you, in the midst of stately councils and the thoughts and memory of you, instead of being an obstacle, has been to me an inspiration."[18] She continued in that role until his death in 1881.

His relationship with Queen Victoria was necessarily of a different nature. She made no secret of the fact that she greatly preferred him to Gladstone. Her husband, Prince Albert, had died in October 1861. When Disraeli paid tribute to him in the House of Commons, the Queen wrote "She could not resist from expressing personally to Mr Disraeli her thanks at the tribute he had paid –the perusal of it had made her shed tears, but it was very soothing to her broken heart."[19] In 1868, when Disraeli became Prime Minster, there started a correspondence and relationship beyond the normal formal communications between a sovereign and a prime minister. Disraeli recognised the loneliness of the Queen and made every effort to flatter and ingratiate himself, with deferential flirtatiousness. He once said "You have heard me called a flatterer. It is true. Everyone likes flattery and, when you come to royalty, you should lay it on with a trowel."[20] She permitted him to sit down during audiences and to write to her in the first person, letters written in the most unctuous and most romantic tone. Her letters to him often ended "Ever yours affectionately. V.R.I." She set him gifts, including a copy of Albert's speeches, bound in white morocco, with an inscription in

18 Aldous, Richard. *The Lion and the Unicorn.* (Hutchinson. London. 2006) pp250-251
19 Hibbert p244
20 Longford, Elizabeth. *Victoria. R.I.* (Weidenfeld and Nicolson. London 1964) p 401

her own hand: "To the Right Honourable Benjamin Disraeli – from the beloved Prince's broken hearted widow. Victoria. R." In 1868, she also sent him a copy of her book, *Leaves from the Journal of our Life in the Highlands.* Disraeli wrote to say that "it possessed a freshness and fragrance like the heather amidst which it was written" and finishing with "We authors, Ma'am."[21]

After one of his visits to Osborne, he wrote to Sarah:

"I can only describe my reception by telling you that I really thought she was going to embrace me. She was wreathed in smiles—she said You ought not to stand now! You shall have a chair!"

This was a very personal favour, because Disraeli remembered being told that the Queen, on one occasion, had had to explain to Lord Derby that, even after his severe illness, she was sorry not to be able to ask him to be seated.[22] She insisted on Disraeli being photographed by her photographer and gave him two volumes of views at Balmoral, a box full of family photographs and a fine portrait of the Prince. As a mark of her personal regard and friendship she also granted him the right to wear the Windsor uniform, worn only by the Royal Family and certain members of the Royal Household.

Some idea of their relationship is to be gathered from a letter he wrote to her at one Christmas:

"Ever since he has been intimately connected with your Majesty, your Majesty has been to him a guardian Angel, and much that he has done that is right, or said that was appropriate is due to you, Madam. He often thinks how he can repay your Majesty, but he has nothing more to give, having given your Majesty his duty and his heart."[23]

When in 1880 he resigned there was mutual grief. He wrote: "His separation from your Majesty is almost overwhelming. His relations with your Majesty were his chief, he might almost say,

21 Bradford p 282
22 Hibbert. (ed) *Queen Victoria Letters and Journals.*(Sutton Publishing Ltd. Stroud. 2000) p 319
23 Monypenny, W.F and Buckle G.E. *The Life of Benjamin Disraeli.* (Macmillan. London. 1929) vol ii p 1342

his only happiness and interest in this world." She replied: "that when we correspond which I hope that we shall on many a *private* matter—without anyone knowing about it, Disraeli would do the same."[24] After resigning he wrote some twenty two letters to her privately, bypassing official channels. One letter read "*Christmas Day* Oh, Madam and most beloved sovereign. What language can express my feelings when I beheld this morning the graceful and gracious gifts upon my table. Such incidents make life delightful and inspire even age with the glow and energy of youth."[25]

When he died, she was overcome with grief. She wrote "I hardly dare trust to speak of myself. The loss is so *overwhelming*— -Never had I so kind and devoted a minister and very few such devoted friends. – but none whose loss will be more keenly felt— God's will be done but the bitterness and suffering are none the less severe."[26] She sent two wreaths of fresh primroses for the coffin with the inscription: "His favourite flowers from Osborne, a tribute of affection from Queen Victoria". She did not attend the funeral but shortly afterwards made a pilgrimage to Hughenden where the vault was reopened and she laid a china wreath of flowers on the coffin.

That Victoria, emotional at the loss of her beloved Albert, was able to find consolation in the somewhat unctuous attentions of a born flatterer tends to suggest that prey and predator both regarded their relationship as mutually satisfactory.

---

24 Ibid vol vi p 527
25 Blake p 724
26 Ibid p752

CHAPTER THREE

GLADSTONE AND WOMEN

Gladstone was Prime Minister of Great Britain four times in the 19th century. On the last occasion he was aged 81, He finally resigned when he was aged 84. Born in 1809, a few years before the Battle of Waterloo, he died in 1898 some years before the Great War. In a political career lasting some 60 years he was also Chancellor of the Exchequer four times. He was described by David Lloyd George, himself a Liberal Prime Minister, as "Head and shoulders above anyone else I have ever seen in the House of Commons—he was far and away the best Parliamentary speaker I have ever heard."[27]

He went to school at Eton and then went on to Christ Church College, Oxford, where he read classics and mathematics. He achieved a first class degree in both subjects. After becoming President of the Oxford Union Debating Society, in 1832 he was elected to be Member of Parliament for Newark. He was at this time a Tory and became a minister under Sir Robert Peel. In 1840 he began the practice which was to continue through his life, of seeking to rescue and rehabilitate prostitutes, walking the streets in London. Disraeli is reputed (almost certainly inaccurately) to have said to Gladstone "When you are out saving fallen women, save one for me." This habit occasioned a good deal of criticism from his peers, though his wife supported him. She was Catherine Glynn whom he married in 1839. This was after two unsuccessful proposals to other women.

---

27 Blake, Robert. *Disraeli* (Eyre and Spttiswoode. London. 1966) p 76

The first was Caroline Farquhar, who was the sister of one of Gladstone's Eton and Christ Church friends. Although he spent time in her company and that of her family he seems not to have shared his affection for her with Caroline herself. Instead he wrote to her father requesting "access to her affections" with a view to marriage. The project was embarked upon rather as one might buy a horse or house.[28] Her mother (Lady Farquhar) wrote to Gladstone: "Caroline expressed surprise at the communication, not having the smallest idea that you entertained any preference for her". When Gladstone replied with a long letter about the importance of his moral and religious views on marriage, Lady Farquhar wrote that "Caroline felt the responsibility too great."[29] Nothing came of the affair though he continued to pursue it.[30] In 1836 she was married to Charles Grey.

His next choice fell on Lady Frances Douglas to whom he proposed by letter. Again this came to nothing, despite his persistent approach to her parents who told Gladstone to stop the correspondence. The family were glad to get her married to Lord Milton.[31] Gladstone's problem seems to have been that he was somewhat gauche, very earnest and full of religious fever for marriage. Happily, in 1839 he married Catherine Glynne. The marriage lasted nearly 60 years.

His involvement with prostitutes began in 1840. He was to set up a number of establishments to help them. His interest in sex had begun at an early age. He recorded occasions in his diaries when he read pornography or visited prostitutes, when he masturbated and when he flagellated himself. These occasions were marked in his diaries with a sign of a small whip or an x when he had read pornography.[32] His idea was that it would discourage, rather than stimulate, sexual excitement but he may well have been deluding himself. His determination to rescue women was not confined to prostitutes.

---

28 Aldous. p 28
29 Isba, Anne, *Gladstone and Women.* (Hambledon Continuum, London 2006) p 23
30 Jenkins, Roy. *Gladstone* (Random House. New York. 1995) p 45
31 Ibid, p 47
32 *Diaries* passim

In 1849, the Countess of Lincoln, married for some 17 years to Gladstone's long standing Eton and Christchurch friend, decided to leave her husband and go and live with Lord Walpole in Italy. Gladstone decided that it was incumbent on him to seek out Lady Lincoln and bring her back to conjugal duty.[33] To this end, he set out for Italy and, after eleven days of travel, reached Naples. From there he went to Milan and then to Como and to various other cities in Italy, without finding Lady Lincoln. He did learn that she was pregnant. He then gave up the struggle, recording in his diary "Oh that poor miserable Lady L—once the dream of dreams, the image that to my young age combined everything that earth could offer of beauty and of joy.—But may that Spotless Sacrifice of whereof I partook, unworthy as I am, today avail for her to the washing away of sin and to the renewal of the image of God."[34]

Between 1840 and 1854, Catherine bore him eight children and at least one miscarriage. Convention of the day was that husbands did not sleep with their wives during pregnancy. He described his fixation on pornography (what he called his besetting sin) in a memorandum in 1845: "The remedies he offered himself to be rid of the fixation included 1. Prayer for blessing of any act to be done. 2. Realising the presence of the Lord, crucified and Enthroned. 3. Immediate pain."[35] It was in 1849 that he first made an entry in his diary indicating self-flagellation and the last entry is in 1859. His involvement with prostitutes had started as early as 1827 and continued in the 1840s, which involved setting up the Margaret Street brotherhood for the redemption of fallen women. But by 1849, he was regularly meeting them late at night and sometimes accompanying them back to their rooms. That it was not all rescue work but had a strong measure of sexual pleasure is clear. On occasions, he described his rescue efforts as "Carnal" and "The chief burden of my soul."[36]

---

33 Jenkins p 93
34 *Diaries*. IV p 144.
35 Aldous p 53.
36 *Diaries* IV pp 319 & 586

Some names appear regularly in his Diaries. He described Emily Collins as "beautiful beyond measure"[37] He had first met her on 11 July, 1850, and was much interested. Thereafter he saw a good deal of her and wrote letters to her. On one occasion he wrote: "I then in a singular way hit upon EC; two more hours, strange, questionable, or more (followed by the sign of the scourge) whether I have been deluded in the notion of doing good by such means, whether I have sought it through what was unlawful, I am not clear. God grant however, not for my sake that the good may be done."[38] On another occasion he wrote: "went with a note to E.C.'s (received unexpectedly) and remained two hours; a strange and humbling scene- returned;" followed by the sign of the scourge.[39] He frequently used phrases such as "weakness", "not all right with me" and "my trusts are carnal."[40] He continued to see her infrequently until January 1854.

Another of the prostitutes he befriended was Emma Clifton. Gladstone used to take up a "beat" oppose the Argyll Rooms in Great Windmill Street, which was a well-known brothel. He spent some time with her in the summer of 1850. He wrote "Saw E. Clifton at night and made, I hope some way.—But alas my unworthiness."[41] Thereafter he seems to have spent much time fruitlessly trying to find her. But, in the spring of 1851, he took up with P. Lightfoot whom, on one occasion, he took back to his new house in Carlton Gardens.[42] After a meeting, his diary records: "my trysts are carnal or the withdrawal would not leave such a void;" "Said I thought it must be the last time as I fear lest more harm was done than good.—I was certainly wrong in some things and trod the path of danger."[43] It wasn't the end. He saw her again in May and October and thereafter sought her out on two or three occasions until 1858.

---

37 Ibid p 440
38 Ibid p346
39 Ibid p344
40 Ibid passim
41 Ibid p 342
42 Aldous. P 53
43 *Diaries* iv p 319

It was in July 1859, that Gladstone first met Marian Summerhayes. She was a courtesan and artists' model and a class above the common prostitutes whom he had previously favoured. He described he in his diary "as full in the highest degree both of interest and of beauty."[44] Gladstone saw her almost daily. He read Tennyson to her and, eight days after their first meeting, he suggested to his friend William Dyce, the Pre-Raphaelite painter, that she should sit for him. In due course she did and the portrait was initially entitled *Lady with a Coronet of Jasmine*. It is now known as *Beatrice*. Gladstone used to write to her when he was not seeing her. He confided in his diary in August: "The case is no common one. May God grant that all go right. To me no trivial matter, for evil or for good".[45]

In September, he obviously had second thoughts about the relationship as his diary recorded: "My thoughts of S require to be limited and purged".[46] Later that month, however, he spent an evening with her reading Tennyson's *Princess* for some four and a half hours. Thereafter he continued to see her regularly until December when she married a man called Dale. He wrote to her in 1860 and thereafter, enquiring about her. In 1880, he destroyed the letters sent to him, observing: "Two of the writers were Mrs Dale — cases of great interest, in qualities as well as attractions, certainly belonging to the flower of their sex. I am concerned to have lost sight of them."[47]

Gladstone's relationship with women involved him in trying, in some cases, to reform them. His wife, Catherine took an active part in this exercise, providing a bed for the night for some of the girls and in other cases trying to place them as domestics in private houses. She also provided help and comfort to the sick and destitute on a regular basis. She could scarcely have been unaware of her husband's fascination with prostitutes but whether she fully appreciated the extent of that interest is unlikely. In January 1854, he had described this in his diary "This morning I lay awake

44 Ibid v p 418
45 Ibid p 421
46 Ibid p 422
47 Isba p 114

– reflecting and counting up the numbers of those unhappy beings, now present to my memory, with whom during now so many years I have conversed indoors and out. I reckoned from eighty to ninety."[48] In July 1851 he had written to Catherine: "How little you know of the evil of my life of which, at the last day I shall a tale to tell".[49]

His affair with Harriet Sutherland was of a totally different nature. Harriet was the granddaughter of Georgina, Duchess of Devonshire. She was, in her own right, a distinguished society hostess at Stafford House and was, for sometime, Mistress of the Robes. She was a few years older than Gladstone and had come out before she was seventeen. She was immensely wealthy and belonged to one of the most important Whig families of the day. It was at Dunrobin Castle, a Sutherland seat, that in 1853 Gladstone and Harriet became close friends. Gladstone was taken seriously ill with an inflammation which lasted over three weeks and Harriet was "full of the utmost kindness and simplicity."[50] Harriet introduced Gladstone at her salons and country weekend parties to influential Liberal figures and gave him support, advice and political solace for the rest of her life which ended in 1868. He frequently visited the Sutherland house at Cliveden. She was a philanthropist and full of religious fervour. There is little evidence that their relationship was other than platonic.

When she died, he was devastated and wrote in his diary: "I have lost the warmest and dearest friend, surely that man ever had. Why this noble and tender spirit should have had such bounty for me and so freshened my advancing years, I cannot tell. But I feel, strange though it might sound, ten years older for her death."[51] He took the view that no one would fill her place. But he was soon to have a relationship of a quite different nature with Laura Thistlethwayte.

It is believed that Laura was born in October 1831 and was thus over 20 years younger than Gladstone. She was beautiful, a

---

48 *Diaries* iv. p 586
49 Isba p100
50 *Diaries* iv pp 3/27
51 *Diaries* viii p 570

former prostitute, and courtesan and subsequently a wife. She had grown up in Ireland, where it is thought she had an affair with Lord Lincoln, then Chief Secretary of Ireland. In May 1850, she was living in London and became the mistress of the Prime Minister of Nepal, who was on a State visit to England. He set her up in a London house, spending a lot of money on her and she followed him when he moved to Paris. When she returned to London she married Captain Frederick Thistlethwayte in 1852. Here she began evangelical preaching. She and Gladstone first met after the death of their mutual friend, Lord Lincoln in 1864. After Harriet's death, he started seeing a lot of Laura and, in 1869, as a result of a request by Gladstone, she sent him copies of her autobiography in separate instalments, designed no doubt to whet his appetite and gain affection. In one letter, he wrote: "I have suffered the pain of parting and very sharp it is; for I think the inner feelings of a woman most sacred; most of all in a case such as that between us".[52] Gladstone had recognised in Mrs Thistlewhayte "an awe-inspiring combination of physical beauty, religious sentimentality and barely repressed immorality."[53]

She sent him gifts including a ring which he regarded as a bond and which he had engraved with the letter "L". The lavish gifts were subsequently to cause some problems for both of them when her husband was sued by a money lender over the gifts, Their correspondence grew more intimate. She invited him to stay in the Thistlewayte rented House in the West Country at Boveridge, without Catherine. There were visits by her to his room alone, both by night and day. In order to go on this amorous assignation, he had adjourned a Cabinet meeting to the following week. He described her as coming to his room "with her hair let down—it is a robe. So Godiva, the rippled ringlets to the knee."[54] His diary entries of their meetings throughout the 1870s were marked with "X". He visited her frequently in London, staying for periods of time, though gradually the relationship grew less frenetic with

---

52 Ibid vii p573
53 Aldous p 208
54 Diaries vii p 578

periods of silence. His diary for April 1870 reads: "It is difficult to repel—the attachment of a remarkable soul, clad in a beautiful body. No matter that the attachment is upright. Whatever be the intention that it shall ever remain so,—still the hold taken is deep."[55]

He was still seeing her in October 1872 when he dined with her twice in London (and stayed late). In March 1873, when Disraeli refused to take office after Gladstone's defeat in the House of Commons, his relationship with Laura intensified. Relations were still active in August 1874.[56] In October 1875, she invited Gladstone to visit her at Lord Bathurst's estate at Oakley Park, Cirencester where they were together for some four days. Of that visit he wrote: "Sat. Saw Mrs T. Visit 1. Sun Evening. Mrs T. no 2. Mon. Mrs T. no.3."[57] This was the second occasion after Boveridge on which writers have assumed that they were lovers and his unannounced visits to her house in London gave rise to much similar speculation.[58]

Whatever Gladstone did or did not do with the numerous prostitutes he accosted on the street, there can be no doubt that it was he that sought them out and not vice versa. He was the predator, though as prey they undoubtedly benefitted from the relationship. His affairs with Harriet and Laura were of a totally different nature. With Harriet it was a joint exercise in friendship, almost certainly of a platonic kind. With Laura, all the indications are that she set out to capture his interest, letting him learn of her background little by little to attract his interest and inducing him to become involved with her. While he may not have needed much encouragement to seize the bait, it was she who essentially made the running and was the predator.

---

55 Ibid p 587
56 Jenkins p 384
57 *Diaries* vol ix 321
58 *Historic Research*. Vol 80. Issue 209 pp 308-392

CHAPTER FOUR

KING EDWARD SEVENTH

Because of their power over life and death, Royal Families have historically been favourite examples of the Aphrodisiac of Power. In more modern times, it is the social power which enables them to attract beautiful women. In the nineteenth century, actresses and chorus girls found themselves being pursued by the aristocracy, sometimes thereby acquiring a title but more often simply being an object of sexual desire and kept for that purpose.

As the leader of the social world, Edward, Prince of Wales, and subsequently, King Edward the Seventh, was in a pivotal position to exercise enormous power and to satisfy his every whim. He was born in December 1841, the second child but the eldest son of Queen Victoria. At the age of seven he started on a private education with a team of tutors. Initially he seems to have been disobedient, ill-mannered and bad tempered.[59] He was subjected to a strict regime of as many as six hours a day of lessons. Eventually Victoria and, more importantly, his father, Prince Albert, realised that Edward need to meet other companions. He was therefore sent off to Eton with his younger brother. There, he seems not to have adapted to the give and take of a Victorian Public school. He appeared to be lacking in that self-reliance, more common among those constantly exposed to the challenges of life. Albert was determined with typical German zeal that his son should be fully prepared for the trials and duties which would someday be his lot. It was decided that, after some coaching at Edinburgh, he should go to Oxford University.

---

59 Magnus, Philip. *King Edward the Seventh.* (John Murray. London 1964) p 7

In October 1859, he became an undergraduate at Christ Church. In the long vacation in 1860, Edward went on a long tour of Canada and the United States. It was an enormously popular visit which did much to enhance Edward's prestige and to instil in him a good deal of self-confidence. After leaving Oxford, he went to Trinity College, Cambridge, where he seems to have led a more social life.

He was keen to join the Guards and it was while he was training with them, that he had his first romance. The object of his affections was an Irish actress called Nellie Clifden who, with the assistance of his brother officers, was smuggled into the camp at the Curragh in order to initiate him into the pleasures of sex. At the same time, Victoria and Albert were in talks to arrange an engagement between Edward and Princess Alexandra, the daughter of Prince Christian of Denmark. In September 1861, Edward travelled to see her and came back with a favourable impression and she was invited to come to England. Meanwhile news of Edward's affair with Nellie Clifden had reached the ears of Albert, who reacted by forgiving Edward for the offence. Within a few days, Albert contracted typhoid and died on 14 December1861. Thereafter, Victoria went into a period of deep mourning which lasted for the rest of her reign. Because Victoria associated Albert's death with his anxiety over Edward's behaviour, he was prudently sent on an extensive holiday abroad.

In October 1862, he met Princess Alexandra again, proposed and they became engaged. On 10 March 1863 they were married. Much to the annoyance of Victoria, Edward and Alexandra started to lead an idle and frivolous social life, having no particular role to play or particular responsibility. He was not to be allowed to represent the Queen or have any official position, although he could open buildings, go to public dinners and visit institutions. When Denmark was invaded by the Prussian and Austrian armies, his request to be able to see the Foreign Office despatches was turned down by Victoria. Nor was he allowed to have access to the red boxes which contained the confidential government documents provided by ministers to the Queen. How did he pass the time? He started to gamble. He hunted and he spent a good deal of time shooting a large number of pheasants on his

Sandringham estate. In January 1870 he found himself called as a witness in divorce proceedings between Sir Charles and Lady Mordaunt. He was accused of committing adultery with Lady Mordaunt, which he denied. He was not cross-examined by Sir Charles' counsel.

Victoria expressed her view about the affair forcefully. She wrote to the Lord Chancellor "Still the fact of the Prince of Wales' intimate acquaintance with a young married woman being publicly proclaimed, will show an amount of imprudence which cannot but damage him in the eyes of the middle and lower classes, which is most deeply to be lamented in these days when the higher classes in their frivolous, selfish and pleasure-seeking lives, do more to increase the spirit of democracy than anything else."[60] Edward's employment still remained a problem and Gladstone, the Prime Minister, carried on a long and eventually fruitless correspondence with Victoria, suggesting that Edward go to Dublin and there act as the Queen's permanent representative. The idea died a death when neither Edward nor Victoria approved of it. Edward therefore continued his idle social life, finding the opportunity to visit France with some frequency. There he took up with two French ladies of society, the Duchesse de Mouchy and the Princesse de Sagan. Another who attracted Edward's attention was Lady Aylesford, but far more serious were his subsequent affairs with Lilly Langtry, the actress Hortense Schneider, the Hon Mrs Keppel and Lady Brooke, later Countess of Warwick.

In May 1877, Edward met Lilly Langtry, a 23 year old married woman, who had taken London Society by storm. Known as the "Jersey Lily", she quickly became Edward's mistress. Both her husband and Alexandra (now mother of a large family) seemed perfectly happy to acquiesce in this arrangement. Lily's husband, whom she had married in 1874, was a 26 year old Irish landowner, and a widower. They had married in Jersey where Lily had been brought up. She had been privately educated and was unusually well educated for women of that time. They moved to London and through the good offices of Lord Ranleigh, a friend

---

60 Ibid p 108

of her father and the painter, Frank Miles, they were introduced to London Society. Here she attracted notice because of her beauty and her wit. Miles made some sketches of her which became very popular on postcards and Sir John Millais painted her portrait, entitling it "The Jersey Lilly". Its appearance at the Royal Academy created something of a sensation. In December 1881 she appeared at the Haymarket theatre in "She Stoops to Conquer." By June 1880, the affair had come to an end though her acting career flourished.

The Prince remained a friend and he continued to use his influence to secure parts for her. In 1879, she had begun affairs with Prince Louis of Battenberg, the Earl of Shrewsbury and Arthur Jones, with whom she carried on a passionate correspondence. The latter was thought to be the father of her daughter, born in 1881. From 1882 until 1891 she had an affair with an American millionaire called Frederic Gebhard and together they ran a number of racehorses in America, where she became a citizen. She also bought a winery in California. In 1899, she married again, to a young race horse owner Hugo de Bathe and they went to live in Monaco where she died in 1929.

Next in line was Hortense Schneider, who was an opera singer of some distinction. When Offenbach wrote "La Grande Duchesse" for the International Exhibition in Paris in 1871, she was the star. It was a satire on German militarism. Half the crowned heads of Europe, including Edward, queued up to pay homage to her and she was nicknamed "le passage des princes". She had created the role of Perichole in Offenbach's satire of the corrupt Court of Louis Napoleon, in the opera of that name. It was first produced in Paris, in October 1868. It was customary for the nobility of this period to have a number of mistresses but, to keep up appearances, they had to be married. Hortense was born in April 1833 in Bordeaux but when she came to Paris she was quickly noticed by Offenbach. She starred successfully in a number of his operettas. She performed in London and St Petersburg to great acclaim. Her relationship with Edward was the subject of much gossip and newspaper reports which his private secretary recorded. She retired in 1878 after her marriage but lived on for another forty years, dying in Paris in 1920.

Daisy Greville, subsequently Countess of Warwick, became Edward's mistress from about 1886. She had been born in 1861 and was considered as a possible bride for Edward's brother, Leopold. Instead she married Francis Greville, Lord Brooke, subsequently to become the Earl of Warwick. In 1886 the couple joined the Prince's inner circle, known as the "Marlborough House Set". Among others who were close companions of Edward were Lord and Lady Charles Beresford. Lord Charles had conducted an affair with Daisy, who, on discovering in 1889 that Lady Charles Beresford was pregnant, wrote, in her fury, an extravagant letter of reproach to Lord Charles. Unfortunately, by accident, it fell into the hands of Lady Charles. She took it to a solicitor, George Lewis, with instructions to ensure that Daisy caused no more trouble between her and her husband. Daisy persuaded Edward to try and retrieve the letter but Lady Charles was not willing to release it unless Daisy agreed to remove herself from London for the season. This Daisy was not willing to do. Daisy now became Edward's mistress. Edward banned Lady Charles from Marlborough House which incensed Lord Charles. He called on Edward and threatened him with violence. Then Lady Charles continued to be excluded socially. Lord Charles threatened to challenge Edward to a duel and Lady Charles threatened to make public Edward's mode of life. Alexandra was much distressed by all the rumours and took herself off to Russia, deliberately missing Edward's fiftieth birthday. Eventually good sense prevailed. Daisy was temporarily excluded from Court. A letter from Edward to Lord Charles brought the dispute to an end. But their close friendship never resumed.

Daisy's relationship with Edward came to an end in 1898, at which time he became involved with Mrs Keppel. Daisy met Joe Laycock, a millionaire, by whom she had two children. But he married Kitty Downshire, the divorced wife of an Irish Marquis. Subsequently to pay off her debts, Daisy threatened to blackmail Edward's son, King George V, by publishing Edward's letters to her, but was stopped by an injunction from so doing. One of

Daisy's failings was her inability to be discreet and she had a habit of boasting of her affairs which, for a royal mistress, was quite unacceptable. She acquired the nickname of "The Babbling Brooke." Daisy joined the Social Democratic Federation in 1904 and took up charitable works. She opposed the First World War, supported the October Revolution and joined the Labour party after the war. She died in 1938.

Alice Keppel became Edward's mistress in 1898 and remained his favourite until he died as King in 1910. At the age of 22, she had married the Hon George Keppel. They came from a titled, landowning background but were by no means wealthy and it was agreed that she should cultivate rich lovers to enjoy a comfortable style of living. George raised no objection to Alice's various liaisons and himself had a number of affairs. They lived in London where, in February 1898, they entertained Edward to dinner and, almost immediately, she became his mistress. She was well-known as a society hostess, was politically astute and extremely beautiful. She had the ability to cope with Edward's rather bored and petulant outlook on life. She was described as "being so charming and wise that she had virtually no enemies". Ministers, too, found her counsel of value and there is no doubt but that she contributed more to Edward's life than simply being a courtesan. The niceties, of course, had to be observed and when Edward visited Alice regularly at her house at East Sutton, Kent, George would discreetly leave. A well paid job for George was found, working for Sir Thomas Lipton and Alice's brother became a groom in waiting in the Royal Household. Sir Ernest Cassel, the well-known banker, was engaged by Edward to advise Alice on her investment with the result that she became a very rich woman.

The long suffering Alexandra suffered the presence of these mistresses with varying degrees of tolerance. She became more and more deaf and was unable fully to enjoy the social life which Edward so much favoured. Her unpunctuality, too, caused friction with Edward, but she seems to have regarded Alice as somebody who was to have a considerable influence over Edward and all to the good. Alice was in fact the perfect Royal mistress, combining the qualities of wife, mother, friend, lover and political adviser.

She lightened the dark moods of his later years. She was much valued by his ministers and, as a well-known Liberal hostess, was able to act as a discreet channel between Edward and the Government. Alexandra was fond of Alice and, when Edward was on his death bed, she was kind enough to invite Alice to see him. After his death, the influence which she had enjoyed, vanished and she was no longer a welcome visitor at Court. She and her husband left England and went to live permanently in Italy, where they both died in 1947.

Edward had spent his many years as Prince of Wales as a fun loving, society man about town, who was desperate to be involved in affairs of state. Victoria, while critical of his behaviour, did little to prepare him for his role as a constitutional monarch. His liaisons and passion for gambling has left a picture of a man, ill-suited to be King. The Royal Baccarat Scandal, in which he was involved did nothing to displace a playboy image. Edward had been a guest at Tanby Croft, while visiting Doncaster Races. In the evening the house party played baccarat, a card game, which was then illegal. One of the guests, Lt Colonel Sir William Gordon-Cumming was thought to be cheating. He signed a document agreeing not to play cards again. This was all meant to be confidential. But the details leaked—(some think it was due to Daisy Brooke) and Sir William brought legal proceedings for slander against the other guests and lost. While Edward was not a party to the action, he was called as a witness. The trial gave rise to much publicity and to adverse comment about his behaviour.

In 1901, when Victoria died, Edward became King. It is now recognised that he played an important part in resolving a number of foreign problems, in particular the rapprochement with France, resulting in the Entente Cordiale. At home, he had to cope with the constitutional crisis, arising out of the dispute between the Government and the House of Lords over the Budget. Alice's wise counsel undoubtedly made a contribution to the success of his foreign and domestic policies. His last Act of State was to require a further general election before consenting to promise to create more peers to prevent the Lords from continuing to obstruct the legislative programme of the Liberal Government.

After he became king, Edward was a thoroughly conscientious sovereign who made pleasure his servant, and not his master, in marked contrast to his previous private life. The dignity of his public life, his immense popularity and charm, and the zest, punctuality and panache with which he performed his duty, forcefully and faithfully until the day he died, enhanced the prestige of the monarch The benefits to both predator and prey are obvious.

CHAPTER FIVE

SIR CHARLES DILKE AND MRS CRAWFORD

In July 1885, Sir Charles Dilke was the Liberal M.P. for Chelsea. He had been a member of Gladstone's administration as President of The Local Government Board. It was a post in the Cabinet which he had held since being appointed in December 1882. In June 1885, the Government were defeated by twelve votes on the Finance Bill, and Gladstone resigned. By the end of the month, Lord Salisbury had formed a minority Government of Tories supported by the Irish vote. It was not expected to last beyond the end of the year and there was much speculation whether Gladstone, now aged seventy five, would retire and hand over the reins to a successor. Dilke had been widely regarded by a number of prominent politicians and commentators as a possible successor, if not immediately, certainly in the foreseeable future. He was still only forty two and in good health. The Radical element of the Liberal Party looked on him and Joseph Chamberlain as their natural leaders. A group of Radicals, who had been in the Cabinet, then met regularly to discuss the future. Dilke thought that Gladstone was in favour of his succession and Chamberlain agreed to Dilke being the front runner.[61]

On 17 July 1885, Mrs Crawford, the wife of Donald Crawford M.P., confessed to her husband that she had committed adultery with Dilke, starting shortly after her marriage to Crawford in 1881, when she was eighteen. Crawford had been the Political

---

61 Jenkins, Roy. *Sir Chares Dilke* (Collins London 1958) p212

Secretary to the Lord Advocate and had been appointed to be one of the Boundary Commissioners to advise on the provisions of the Redistribution Bill, concerned with changes to the voting franchise. Dilke was cited as co-respondent to Crawford's divorce petition, but, on 12 February1886, Mr Justice Butt dismissed Dilke from the case and awarded him his costs against Crawford. On 23 July, before the President of the Probate, Divorce and Admiralty division of the High Court, Sir James Hannen, a jury decided that Mrs Crawford's confession was truthful and that, accordingly, Dilke had indeed committed adultery with Mrs Crawford. Dilke's political career was now in tatters and although he was, later, to become an MP again, he was never to be offered or to hold any political post. .What had caused such a dramatic fall from power?

Dilke was born on 4 September 1843, six years after Queen Victoria came to the throne and died on 26 January, 1911. Wentworth Dilke, Dilke's father, was involved in Exhibitions and was made a baronet by the Queen in 1862. For three years he had been a Liberal M.P. for Wallingford. But his influence on Dilke was minimal. In 1853, Dilke's mother died. Dilke looked to his grandfather for support and education. He never went to school because it was thought that he did not have sufficient strength and was of a nervous disposition. He had some private tuition and did some work at a local day school. At an early age, he was a regular playgoer and, with his grandfather, travelled extensively, particularly in France. He was to become an enthusiastic Francophile with many distinguished French friends. In 1862, he went up to Trinity Hall, Cambridge where he took up rowing seriously and was in their first boat for three years He read mathematics in his first year and won a college scholarship. He then changed to read law. He won a college law prize. In two successive years he won the College English essay prize and he was also honoured by being the Senior Legalist, the most prestigious University award for a law student. This was based on a determination to acquire knowledge –"and this remained his approach throughout life."[62] He had the further distinction of becoming President of the Cambridge Union in 1864.

---

62 Ibid p 26

He spent the next year travelling round the world, about which he wrote much in his book containing his political philosophy, *Greater Britain*. At the same time he was adopted as Liberal candidate for the borough of Chelsea. His views were essentially radical. When the General Election took place in November 1868, he was elected with a substantial majority. The Liberal party under Gladstone had a sizeable majority. Thereafter, he was a constant thorn in the side of the Government, aligned as he was with others of strong radical views. Among the leaders of this group was Joseph Chamberlain whose family had strong connections with Birmingham. He and Dilke formed a political alliance and eventually, a social friendship.

In the 1870s Dilke set himself up as a champion of Republicanism. Queen Victoria's withdrawal from all public duties after the death of her husband and the Prince of Wales' attachment to loose living in London and elsewhere, did nothing to enhance the popularity of the monarchy. Dilke's views are encapsulated in a speech which he made Newcastle on Tyne in November 1871 when he said: "if you can show me a fair chance that a republic here will be free from the political corruption which hangs about the monarchy, I say, for my part—and I believe that the middle classes in general will say—let it come."

In 1872, he married Katherine. They had one son. In 1874 she died and, in February 1875, Dilke renewed an old friendship with Emilia Pattison which led eventually to their getting married in 1885. His political reputation grew rapidly and even opponents were forecasting a great future for him. Lord Beaconsfield, who as Disraeli, had been Gladstone's political adversary, pronounced that Dilke was not only the most useful member, among quite young men, that he had ever known, but also that he was almost certain to be Prime Minister. He was also described as the only successful young man that Parliament had produced in recent years.[63]

When in April 1880, the Liberals won the election with Gladstone as Prime Minister, there was a dispute between

---

63 Jenkins pp 102 & 118

Chamberlain and Dilke about joining the Cabinet, as a result of which Chamberlain became President of the Board of Trade with a seat in the Cabinet while Dilke was offered and accepted the under-secretaryship at the Foreign Office. In December 1882, as a result of a Cabinet reconstruction, Dilke now became President of the Local Government Board at the age of thirty nine, the youngest member of the Cabinet. By 1884, Gladstone's administration was beginning to die. The murder of Gordon, problems over Ireland, disagreements about the Budget and anxiety about Russian activity in Afghanistan all conspired to weaken the Government and to lead to its defeat on a vote in June 1884. Speculation as to whether Gladstone would resign and, if so, when, led many to believe that Dilke would take over leadership of the Liberal party. But any question of that was quickly resolved by Gladstone' determination to remain in power and by the impact of Mrs Crawford's allegation of adultery with Dilke.

Mrs Crawford was born in 1863. Her father was a ship repairer at Tyneside, whose father had been the founder of Smiths' Docks. There were seven daughters in the family of ten children. They lived partly in London and partly in Northumberland. Photos of her at the time of the trial show her to be an attractive young girl. She had been educated in France at a convent. She was not a Catholic but after the trial, in 1889, she converted to Catholicism. On her return from France, at the age of seventeen, she did the season and, in 1881, married Donald Crawford. It is suggested that she did this not out of love, but to escape from an overbearing mother. On 17 July, 1885, Donald Crawford, as he subsequently told Mr Justice Butt, found an anonymous letter when he arrived at his home in George Street. This was the last in a series of anonymous letters which he had received about the conduct of his wife. The first note was in the spring of 1882. Apart from warning Crawford that his wife, on a visit to a hospital, had been flirting with medical students, the note went on to add "Beware of the member for Chelsea" (i.e. Dilke). The next note in March 1885, accused Mrs Crawford of being Dilke's mistress. It added that she was well known to the servants at Dilke's house at 76 Sloane Street, where she was a frequent visitor. There, it was alleged that she shared a bed, not only with Dilke, but also at the same time, with a servant girl called Fanny.

The next note, in June 1885, observed that Mrs Crawford had had lunch at the Hotel Metropole with a Captain Forster. The anonymous note which Crawford received in July 1885 read: "Fool, looking for the cuckoo when he has flown. Having defiled your nest. You have been vilely deceived, but you dare not touch the real traitor." When challenged by Crawford, Mrs Crawford told him that she had indeed defiled his bed and that it was not Captain Forster. She said "The man who ruined me was Charles Dilke." Crawford then started divorce proceedings naming Dilke as a co-respondent. The evidence at that stage against him, apart from two minor witnesses, depended entirely on Mrs Crawford's confession. It was the detail of Mrs Crawford's confession about sharing a bed with Fanny, which transformed a simple allegation of adultery by a husband against his wife, into a sensational and scandalous public spectacle. For Dilke, the result was nothing less than a catastrophe.

At the trial before Mr Justice Butt, Mrs Crawford did not give evidence. Her confession was sufficient evidence to enable Crawford to get a divorce. It was not, by reason of the rules of evidence, any evidence against Dilke, unless Mrs Crawford herself gave evidence on oath. Dilke was not obliged as a matter of law to give evidence though as will be seen, as a matter of protecting his reputation, he would have been well advised so to do. The Crawfords and the Dilkes were related by marriage. Mrs Crawford's younger sister, Maye Smith was the wife of Ashton Dilke, Dilke's brother. Thus Dilke and Mrs Crawford were brother and sister in law to each other. The story which Mrs Crawford told Crawford, and which he repeated to the Court, was that in 1861, when she was eighteen, and married, Dilke had called on her at a hotel in the Gloucester Road and they had made love there. Subsequently they had met at a house off Tottenham Court Road and thereafter for a period of some two and a half years until summer 1884, she and he frequently committed adultery at Dilke's house in Sloane Street and at Crawford's in Kensington.

Thus far there was nothing outside the familiar tale of a lover and his mistress. What attracted public excitement and condemnation was the further evidence which Mrs Crawford admitted.

It was to the effect that, at Sloane Square, there was a servant called Sarah who she thought had been Dike's mistress and a Mrs Rogerson who fell into the same category. In addition Dilke had been a lover of Mrs Crawford's mother. Further, said Mrs Crawford, there was another servant girl in the house, of the same age as her, called Fanny who spent every night with Dilke. Dilke was keen to have a threesome. After an initial reluctance by Mrs Crawford, she eventually succumbed and the three of them shared the same bed. To add to this revelation, she said "He taught me every French vice and I knew more than most women of thirty." An attempt by Dilke to persuade Mrs Crawford to withdraw her allegations failed. At the end of Crawford's evidence and that of his two supporting witnesses, although it was open to Dilke to go into the witness box and deny Mrs Crawford's evidence on oath, there was as a matter of law no admissible evidence against him of having committed adultery with Mrs Crawford.

Dilke was represented by a formidable legal team led by Rt Hon Sir Henry James, QC, formerly the Attorney General and Sir Charles Russell QC, currently the Attorney General, and widely regarded as one of the greatest advocates of all time at the English Bar. They decided, as lawyers, that, as there was no admissible evidence against Dilke, to leave the case as it stood and not to put Dilke in the witness box. It was a mistake of monumental proportions, aggravated by the explanation which Russell gave to the Court for their decision. "Ought we," he said " to take on the responsibility of putting Sir Charles Dilke in the witness box where he might be put through the events of his whole life, and in the life of any man there may be found to have been some indiscretions—ought we to take on that responsibility? After an anxious consideration of the matter we have come to the determination to leave the case where it stands." If any explanation for the course which they took was appropriate (no explanation was in fact necessary), it was singularly ineptly phrased. However, the Judge thought that counsel had given wise advice and dismissed the case against Dilke with costs.

While Dilke's initial reaction was one of relief, attacks by newspapers, particularly by the Pall Mall Gazette, started to have their effect on public opinion who couldn't understand why Mrs Crawford could be found guilty of adultery with Dilke, while, at the same time, Dilke was acquitted of adultery with Mrs Crawford. Dilke therefore decided to try and upset the verdict by applying to be reinstated in the case, The Court of Appeal rejected his application. He then asked the Queen's Proctor to intervene to challenge the verdict. The Queen's Proctor was Sir Augustus Stephenson. He was an Official whose responsibility was to ensure that divorce proceedings were properly conducted. It required him, in this case, to consider whether Mrs Crawford had indeed committed adultery with Dilke. Dilke was now simply a witness to be called by the Queen's Proctor and did not have the presence of his former legal team to cross examine Mrs Crawford.

Under fierce cross examination by Henry Matthews QC, on behalf of Crawford, Dilke made a poor showing in the witness box. He was one of those witnesses who wouldn't answer yes or no to a simple question and insisted on giving involved, and detailed, explanation for matters suggested to him. In particular, he was asked about the indiscretions to which Russell had made reference at the first trial. Sir Walter Phillimore, on behalf of the Queen's Proctor, was an indifferent advocate and Stephenson showed himself to be lacking in impartiality and gave no help to Dilke's side. Fanny, about whom the sensational evidence had been given at the first trial, was not produced as a witness, although Dilke denied that she was his mistress or had ever been in his bed with or without Mrs Crawford. Mrs Crawford gave evidence on oath, repeating much of what she had said to her husband. Some important pieces of evidence changed substantially, including the fact that she had committed adultery with Captain Forster starting in 1884.

When Mathews made his final address to the Jury, he made much of the fact that Dilke had not given evidence at the first trial. He said "The judge who tried the case had rightly decided that there was no legal evidence against Sir Charles Dilke. But was there not moral evidence of the strongest kind against him? He was charged by Mrs Crawford's confession not merely with adultery, but with having committed adultery with one friend and the wife of another. He was charged with having committed with Mrs Crawford, ruthless adultery unredeemed by love or affection—he was charged with coarse, brutal, adultery, more befitting a beast than a man; he was charged with having done with an English Lady what any man of proper feeling would shrink from doing with a prostitute in a French brothel, and yet he was silent." It was a powerful and effective piece of advocacy. Unsurprisingly the jury retired for no more than a quarter of an hour before returning a verdict that effectively convicted Dilke of having committed adultery with Mrs Crawford. In the light of some of the unsatisfactory evidence given by Mrs Crawford, a Committee was set up on Dilke's behalf to carry out further investigation. The result showed that Mrs Crawford had lied about the date when she had first committed adultery with Forster, and had lied about adultery with others. But it availed Dilke not at all. He was therefore left to pick up the pieces as best he could. On 3 October 1885, in the middle of Crawford's allegations, he married Emilia Pattison who had been his mistress. They had a happy married life until she died in 1904.

Politically, his career for the moment stood still. He had lost his Chelsea seat in the election of 1886. Thereafter, he was offered two or three seats but turned them down. However, in 1889, the Liberals in the Forest of Dean expressed an interest in a visit by Dilke and his first visit was a great success. He needed the approval of Gladstone, which he received, with the qualification that Dilke should wait until the next General Election. By 1891, when Dilke accepted an invitation to be the Liberal candidate at the Forest of Dean, a mining constituency, Gladstone had changed his mind. This was the effect of the divorce proceedings, involving Charles Parnell, the leader of the Irish national party who had committed adultery with Kitty O'Shea. He was a strong supporter of Gladstone's. To have two adulterers supporting the Liberal party was a step too far for Gladstone. In the summer of 1892, however Dilke was returned to Parliament and he remained the member for the rest of his life. A government post was not offered by Gladstone. Thereafter a succession of Liberal defeats meant that there was no office available for him. During the years thereafter, among other activities, Dilke immersed himself in military affairs, particularly Imperial Defence. He had written *The British Army* in 1888 and *Imperial Defence* in 1891. When, in 1906, Campbell Bannerman became Prime Minister, Dilke, in view of his military experiences, had hopes that he might be offered the War Office. It was not to be. Nor, when Asquith took over as Prime Minister, was there any further offer. In January 1911, Dilke died. It was a waste of a great talent but politicians never learn.

CHAPTER SIX

CHARLES PARNELL AND
KITTY O'SHEA

The romance between Charles Parnell, the leader of the Irish National Party and Kitty O'Shea, the wife of Captain O'Shea MP was to have an important impact, not only on their own lives, but much more importantly on the future of Anglo Irish relations It is not too much of an exaggeration to take the view that the whole history of Anglo Irish relations after 1890, would have taken a quite different course if there had been no romance and would probably have resulted in a peaceful and permanent settlement of the Irish problem. The troubles which afflicted Ireland thereafter, resulted in much anguish, much loss of life and much hatred. The deep seated wounds are only now gradually beginning to heal and may never be completely removed. Ireland had been subdued by Cromwell in the 17th Century. The land had been given to English landlords by successive English rulers, Elizabeth 1, James 1, and Cromwell, so that the Irish population were simply tenants and had no security of tenure. The land was agricultural and there was little in the way of manufacturing industry. The English landlords were predominantly absentee and primarily concerned with ensuring a proper return on their properties. Rents were at the mercy of market forces and a depression would result in unpaid rent and consequential eviction. Added to the normal hazards of living at a subsistence level, was the ever real possibility of a crop failure.

In 1845, there was partial failure and in 1846 and 1848 there was the total failure of the potato crop. It became known as the Great Famine. Repeal of the Corn Laws had the effect of reducing agricultural prices so that landowners converted their properties into pasture. The famine legacy led to the formation of a number of Irish societies, determined to assert their rights and to resist what they regarded as intolerable English control. The chief progenitor of this Irish nationalism was the Irish Republican Brotherhood, a Fennian movement, who believed in armed revolt. The leaders of the Catholic Church gave them no support. Other groups believed in constitutional reform. One such was the Home Rule League, led by Isaac Butt.

A Fennian revolt in 1867 was put down and the ringleaders arrested and sent for substantial periods of penal servitude. Later, a prison van carrying two Fennians from court to a gaol in Manchester was ambushed and during the attempt to rescue the prisoners, a Police Officer was shot. Three of those involved were arrested, tried and hanged. In 1870, the cry of "Home Rule for Ireland" which became the watchword of the Nationalists was first mooted. Irish tactics were based on political pressure as well as on the threat of violence. For the former it was necessary for the Irish to have representation at Westminster and for there to be established an Irish party to lead the campaign. Parnell became that leader. Initially the tactics were to obstruct the work of government by constant objections, frequent and interminable speeches and irrelevant amendments to legislation. More bad harvests in 1877 and in 1878, together with the failure of the potato crop in 1880, caused further distress. American competition reduced the agricultural prices in Ireland. Additionally there was less demand by English farmers for seasonal Irish labourers and failure to pay rent still resulted in eviction.

A Land League was launched in 1879 to help the tenant farmers and to try to secure some form of security for them. In 1880, the Liberals under Gladstone returned to power. Parnell was re-elected an MP and became President of the Land League and leader of the Irish parliamentary party. The effect of the House of Lords rejecting a modest measure of compensation for disturbance to some tenants, was to cause further outbreaks of violence in Ireland. The Government sought to deal with it by passing a Coercion Act. More importantly, Gladstone introduced a Land Act, which became law in 1881. It was the start of a determined approach by Gladstone to solve the Irish problem.

The Act was designed to ensure some degree of security, a fair rent and the right, for the tenant, freely to sell his interest in his holding. Parnell could not properly reject the provision but foresaw that its implementation would result in the collapse of the League. When, to impress his supporters in Ireland, he spoke vehemently against the Act, the Government had him imprisoned. Violence continued. After six months in gaol, he and Gladstone arrived at an accord, known as the "Kilmainham Treaty". Its effect was that, in exchange for the Government making various concessions on the Land Bill, Parnell agreed to use his influence to restrain further outbreaks of violence in Ireland. Parnell's support among some of his supporters, upset by what they saw as a rejection of social change, was restored when Gladstone reintroduced further coercion. This followed the assassination of the Irish Chief Secretary, Lord Frederick Cavendish and Thomas Burke, a senior official, in Phoenix Park. By 1882, a new body called the Irish National League had been formed and Parnell became its leader. They now had a well disciplined and well organised party who held the balance of power in the House of Commons.

Unfortunately, in June 1885, the Liberal Government lost a debate by twelve votes and resigned, with the Parnellites voting against the Government. The Unionists won the subsequent election, with the Irish in England, voting against the Liberals. But the Unionists only had a majority of two over the Liberals and Irish. Parnell had a great triumph at the election, and his supporters now numbered 85. To secure their support, the Irish had been promised by the Unionists that they would repeal the Coercion Acts. The Irish further hoped to come to some arrangement with the Unionists about a Home Rule Bill for Ireland. However, the Unionists resiled from this undertaking. They announced that they would introduce a new Coercion bill and would seek to suppress the Irish National League. In January 1886, on an amendment to the Queen's speech, the Unionists were defeated and the Liberals under Gladstone returned to power.

Now was the great opportunity for a Home Rule Bill and negotiations began. In April 1886, Gladstone introduced his first Home Rule Bill. Chamberlain, notionally a member of the Government, encouraged his supporters to vote against the bill which was lost by some thirty votes. Parliament was again dissolved and there was another General Election. Although the Irish supported the Liberals, the Unionists won convincingly and, once again, the Home Rule Bill was put on the backburner. But increasingly the Liberals won by-elections and the supporters of Chamberlain started to support Gladstone. The prospects looked good for the return of the Liberals and another chance of a Home Rule Bill. Parnell was now at the height of his powers. He had successfully defeated allegations published in *The Times*, in 1887, that he was complicit to murder. The letters, alleged to have been written by him were shown to be a forgery and he received £5,000 by way of compensation from *The Times*. But on December 24, 1889, Parnell was served with divorce papers naming him as a co-respondent by Captain O'Shea. He was never to recover his pre-eminence and the prospects for Home Rule were set back for generations.

Charles Stewart Parnell was born on June 17, 1846. He came from an aristocratic family, but one which was impeccably anti-British. They lived at Avondale in County Wicklow, Ireland, but had other estates. His mother was American, who was the daughter of Commodore Charles Stewart of the United States Navy, a hero of the US war against the British in 1812. On his father's side he had a distinguished lineage. In the 17th Century, the family acquired land in Queen's County, Ireland. One of his ancestors was Chancellor of the Exchequer in the Irish Parliament; another was Secretary of State for War in the English Parliament and was subsequently to be elevated to the House of Lords. Others were fierce champions of the Irish cause. His father was non-political, a man of leisure who rode to hounds and was a keen cricketer. Parnell had a number of brothers and sisters. For a time his education was mainly at the hands of private teachers. At the age of 13, when his father died, he inherited Avondale. At 15, he was sent to school in England and then received an award at

Magdelene College, Cambridge, where he spent four years, before being sent down. He had an affair with a girl there called Daisy, whom he had seduced. When he gave her up, she drowned herself in the river Cam. Thereafter, he led an idle, sporting life, as befitted an Irish aristocrat. His first romance arose out of a visit to Paris in 1870, where he met an American girl, Miss Woods and they fell in love. It came to nothing. Both she and her parents thought that, not only, was he not rich, but that he lacked any sort of distinction and had achieved nothing. He then spent a year with his brother in America returning in 1872.

In 1874 he had his first attempt at politics, applying to represent County Dublin on a Home Rule ticket in the English Parliament. He was unsuccessful. In 1875, he stood as the candidate for Meath and, in April, he was elected with a large majority. His made no great impression in his first year, but with the Irish becoming disenchanted with the idea of a peaceful resolution of their problems, a policy of obstructing proceedings in Parliament was now adopted as a means of getting a serious hearing about Home Rule. Additionally, the Land League of which Parnell was President, was active in promoting the case for land reform. In 1880 the return of the Liberals suggested a step in the right direction for Home Rule. It was the same year that Parnell became the lover of Kitty O'Shea.

She was the same age as Parnell. Her father was an English vicar and a baronet. Her mother was the daughter of a Portugese Admiral who had been appointed bedchamber woman to the Queen. Kitty's brother became a distinguished Field Marshal and her uncle had been Lord Chancellor. They were not only a distinguished family but were essentially upper-class, living comfortably in a large country mansion, called Rivenhall Place. When she was 18, she met Captain William O'Shea, an officer in the 18th Hussars. In January 1867, they were married. O'Shea soon left the Army and embarked on a number of unsuccessful business ventures. They had a son and two daughters. They were rescued from total penury with the help of some of her relatives. The marriage did not prosper. He liked to spend his time in London while she lived in a house in Eltham, provided by her aunt, Mrs Benjamin Wood. He did not provide for her. Her tastes and interests were superior to his and it became a marriage of convenience. Notwithstanding, his total lack of any qualifications and without any significant career behind him, in 1880, O'Shea decided to enter politics and became a member of Parliament for County Clare.

O'Shea wanted Kitty to give some dinner parties to introduce him to the other Irish members. Kitty invited Parnell on more than one occasion but, when he had not replied, she determined to face him out. In July 1880, when the House of Commons was sitting, she left a written message for him to meet in the Palace Yard. He apologised, saying that he would come to dinner again, if asked. He appeared ill having spent some time in America trying to raise money for the cause. A rose which she was wearing, dropped and was picked up by Parnell, and was in his private papers when he died. He then attended a small dinner party at which O'Shea was not present. Thereafter, he wrote numerous letters to her. The first, dated 17 July reads—"My Dear Mrs O'Shea, We have all been in such a "disturbed "condition lately that I have been quite unable to wander further from here than a radius of about one hundred paces allons. And this, notwith-standing the powerful attractions which have been tending to seduce me from my duty towards my country in the direction of Thomas's Hotel" (which was where Kitty gave dinner parties). She described subsequently how they became lovers: "After this dinner party I met him frequently in the Ladies' Gallery of the House.—whenever I went, he came up for a few minutes; and if the Wednesday sittings were not very important nor required his presence, he would ask me to drive with him. We drove many miles this way in a hansom cab, out into the country, to the river at Mortlake or elsewhere."[64] There was not only a romantic attachment on her part, but she was also motivated by the hope of advancing her husband's political career.

On 9 September, he wrote again, this time from Dublin: "I may tell you in confidence that I don't feel quite so content at

---

64 Katherine O'Shea. *Charles Stewart Parnell.* vol 1(Cassell and Company, Ltd. London. 1914) p 139

the prospect of ten days' absence from London, amongst the hills and valleys of Wicklow as I should have done some three months since. The cause is mysterious, but perhaps you will help me to find it or her, on my return"[65] Two days later he wrote again: "—I am still in the land of the living, notwithstanding the real difficulty of either living or being, which every moment becomes more evident, in the absence of a certain kind and fair face." Ten days later he wrote from Dublin: "I cannot keep myself away from you any longer, so I shall leave tonight for London— I hope to see you tomorrow."[66] Because her old nurse was dying, the meeting had to be postponed to Parnell's disappointment, which gave rise to further correspondence. On 29 September, he wrote: "I propose to visit London again and renew my attempt to gain a glimpse of you—I shall be intensely delighted to have a wire from you to meet me."[67] In the autumn, Parnell was ill and Kitty ministered to him at the house in Eltham, from which O'Shea was notably absent. In one letter from Dublin, Parnell enquired: "Is it true that Captain O'Shea is in Paris, and if so, when do you expect him to return?"[68] On 2 October, he wrote from Dublin: "somehow or other, something from you seems a necessary part of my daily existence and if I have to go a day or two without even a telegram it seems dreadful."[69]

On 17 October, he wrote: "My own love,—You cannot imagine how much you have occupied my thoughts all day and how very greatly the prospect of seeing you again very soon comforts me—".[70] He followed this up a few days later when he wrote on 22 October: "I send you enclosed, one or two poor sprigs of heather, which I plucked for you three weeks ago, also my best love, and hope you will believe that I always think of you as the one dear object whose presence has ever been a great

---

65 Ibid p 142
66 Ibid p 143
67 Ibid p 146
68 Ibid p152
69 Ibid p 152
70 Ibid p 153

42

happiness to me."[71] In December and January 1881, he was writing to her as "My dearest wife", "My dearest love" and "My dearest wifie."[72] In April, he ended one his letters: "Always your husband". O'Shea could scarcely have been unaware of Parnell's frequent visits to Kitty at Eltham, when he was not present, or of her meetings with him at the House of Commons. This was to give rise to much speculation during the divorce proceedings as to whether, for whatever reason, he had connived at their activities. By 1881, she and Parnell were hopelessly in love with one another, while she and O'Shea were leading quite separate lives. On one occasion, O'Shea, finding Parnell's belongings at Eltham, removed them and challenged Parnell to a duel. Happily it never took place. Meanwhile the Government had had enough of what they regarded as sedition and decided to arrest the leading members of the League.

Parnell told Kitty of his arrest in a letter on 13 October: "My own Queenie I have just been arrested and write these words to tell her that she must be a brave little woman and not fret after her husband. The only thing that makes me worried and unhappy is that it may hurt you and our child. You know, darling, that on this account it will be wicked for you to grieve, as I can never have any other wife but you, and if anything happens to you I must die childless. Be good and brave, dear little wifie, then. Your own husband."[73] The reference to "our child" relates to Kitty's pregnancy at this time. A child was born on 16 February 1882 but died two months later. Parnell believed the baby was his, as did Kitty. O'Shea believed he was the father. Kitty gave birth to two further children in 1883 and 1884, of whom there seems little doubt that Parnell was the father. In early May, as a result of what came to be known as the "Kilmainham Treaty", Parnell was released. The arrangements whereby Parnell was released in exchange for a promise by him to adopt a conciliatory attitude towards the Government policies in Ireland gave rise to

71 Ibid p 154
72 Ibid pp 169 & 170
73 Ibid p 207

considerable controversy among his supporters. However, the murders of Lord Frederick Cavendish and Mr Burke in Phoenix Park resulted in the Government introducing a Crimes Bill and once again Ireland was in turmoil.

Parnell now became leader of The Irish National Party and there was comparative calm until 1884. During that year, Parnell and Kitty regularly met and, when absent from each other, wrote letters or sent telegrams. In 1885, when she had a new room built on to the house at Eltham, Parnell superintended every detail and it was turned into his study and workshop.[74] In the autumn of 1885, there was to be another election. The relationship between O'Shea and Parnell worsened. O'Shea had been hoping for political advancement by acting as a go-between, between Parnell and Chamberlain in relation to a scheme of self-government in Ireland. When that ceased to be viable, O'Shea sought a seat in the House of Commons, to represent Liverpool. This came to nothing and Parnell forced him to take the Galway constituency, to the dismay of many of the Irish party. O'Shea had already sought re-election for County Clare with no success, because of his close friendship with Chamberlain. O'Shea thought that Parnell had failed him, because he had promised to give him support and, because he believed that he, O'Shea, had rendered great service to Parnell in regard to the "Kilmainham Treaty." In the event, O'Shea succeeded in being elected as MP for Galway.

1886 saw the first complaint by O'Shea about Kitty's friendship with Parnell. In May, a reference in a newspaper to the fact that Parnell had a suburban retreat in Eltham caused O'Shea to question Kitty who denied any impropriety. It did not prevent Parnell and Kitty from having a seaside holiday together at Eastbourne and taking a three year lease on a seaside house after doing some house hunting, together. O'Shea continued to pursue the allegations against Kitty. In December she wrote to him: "I am perfectly disgusted with your letter. It is really too sickening after all I have done. The only person who has ever tarnished your honour has been yourself you use such disgusting and ungrateful

74 Vol 2 p 74

expressions about me." In December, O'Shea reacted to various rumours in the press by writing to the editor of the Pall Mall Gazette, W. Stead: "It was stated in the Pall Mall Gazette yesterday that Mr Parnell was staying on a visit with me. The fact is that I have had no communication whatsoever with Mr Parnell since May." Stead referred to reports about Parnell's relations with Kitty in a letter he wrote to O'Shea in April 1887: "What I asked you to advise Mrs O'Shea about was this: that reports being wide and strong as to her relations with Mr Parnell, it would, for her children's sake, be expedient that she should declare her renunciation of communication with him."[75] There was some evidence that Parnell was calling himself Mr Fox and also Mr Clement Preston and that, on one occasion, he had escaped from the sudden arrival of O'Shea at a house in Brighton by escaping down a fire escape.

O'Shea was in something of a dilemma about launching divorce proceedings. Mrs Benjamin Wood, Kitty's aunt was a wealthy lady, close to death and a divorce might have cut him out of her will. Secondly, as a Catholic, he needed the benefit of the church's support. When Mrs Benjamin Wood died, leaving everything to Kitty, not only the family challenged the will but also O'Shea. On December 24 1889, however O'Shea did launch divorce proceedings, naming Parnell as co-respondent. By all accounts, Parnell was relaxed about the proceedings and let it be known that he would be successful in his defence.[76] This mistaken view seems to have been built on the belief that O'Shea could be bought off or that Kitty's initial defence of connivance would succeed. That depended on their showing that O'Shea knew of their adultery and accepted it. O'Shea could not be bought off and Kitty's defences were soon abandoned. In any event Parnell wanted the divorce so that he could marry Kitty. Conspiracy theories abound in cases of scandal and there is a view

75 Ibid p 219
76 Abels, Jules. *The Parnell Tragedy*. (The Bodley Head, London.1966) pp 316-320 Lyons. F.S.L. *The Fall of Parnell*. (Routledge & Keegan Paul Ltd. London) pp 39-41. 67 -71

that Chamberlain urged O'Shea to refuse any offer to withdraw because he, Chamberlain, was anxious to destroy Parnell.[77]

Neither Parnell nor Kitty took any part in the divorce proceedings. The evidence, according to Mr Justice Butt, showed that they had sought disguises, and had used subterfuges and evasions to conceal their liaison. He described Parnell as a "man who takes advantage of the hospitality offered him by the husband to debauch the wife". A decree nisi was granted. Custody of the children was awarded to O'Shea and Parnell was ordered to pay costs. The political fallout from the divorce was immediate and catastrophic for Parnell personally and for the future of Home Rule. At a meeting at Leinster Hall on 18 November, a few days after the divorce, there was strong support for Parnell among his Irish colleagues and Healey expressed the view "that for Ireland and for Irishmen, Mr Parnell is less a man than an institution". Elsewhere there was much condemnation. The Church took the lead and was followed by Gladstone and the Liberals. They let Parnell know, through an intermediary, that his continued leadership would be productive of consequences, disastrous in the highest degree, to the cause of Ireland. The letter was duly published.

But Parnell was determined to stay and, on 28 November, issued a manifesto. In it, he claimed that Gladstone had made various private promises which would have seriously damaged Irish expectations. He accused the Liberals of using the divorce as an excuse to avoid commitment to Home Rule. It was not only Gladstone who reacted violently to Parnell's disclosure of private conversations with him. Irish supporters in America drafted a counter manifesto strongly criticising Parnell. Gladstone was not prepared to make any concession about Home Rule until Parnell was removed.

A series of meetings of the Irish party followed. On 6 December, the Irish Nationalist party split. Only 26 members stayed with Parnell. A by-election at Kilkenny on 22 December was to be a test of his leadership in Ireland. It resulted in the

---

77 Abels pp 315-316

defeat of his candidate. Attempts by Parnell to negotiate with Gladstone– "The Boulogne Negotiations" – came to nothing. Another by-election at North Sligo in April 1891 and at Carlow, in July, resulted in defeat for Parnell's candidate. The internal battle for the soul of the party continued with increasing bitterness among its members. Only his marriage to Kitty, on 25 June 1891, brought consolation to Parnell. In the General Election in 1892, the Parnellites won only nine seats out of eighty one. The Liberal vote was much reduced and they were dependent on the Irish vote. Gladstone's Home Rule Bill passed the Commons by 43 votes but was defeated in the Lords. The cause of Irish Nationalism was put back for over a century. Parnell died on 6 October 1891. His last words were "Kiss me sweet wifie and I will try to sleep a little."[78] If ever there were an example of a politician sacrificing his political ambitions for the sake of private pleasure, it was the sad case of Parnell.

---

78 Katherine O'Shea. p 276

CHAPTER SEVEN

ASQUITH AND VENETIA STANLEY

In 1912, Herbert Henry Asquith had been Prime Minister of England for some four years. He was now aged sixty. He had been married twice. By his first wife Helen, he had five children, Raymond, Herbert, Arthur, Violet (later Violet Bonham Carter) and Cyril. After the death of his first wife, he married Margot Tennant in 1894 and together they had five children, of whom only two, Anthony and Elizabeth survived. Venetia Stanley in 1912 was aged 24, the same age as Violet who was a great friend. Between 1912 and May 1915, Asquith wrote over 560 letters of the most passionate nature to Venetia and she replied in kind. They only ceased when she became engaged to Edwin Montagu.

Whether the relationship between Asquith and Venetia was a physical one has been the subject of much debate and no little controversy. That he was deeply in love with her and completely besotted by her is not in doubt.[79] The letters make that abundantly clear. In April 1915, he wrote "Chapter of Autobiography". In it he observed: "The first stage of our intimacy (in which there was not a touch of romance and hardly of sentiment) came to its climax when I went to Sicily with Montagu as a companion, I think at the end of 1911 or the beginning of 1912. Violet and Venetia joined us there and we had together one of the most interesting and delightful fortnights of our lives. It was when we had got back to England I was sitting with her in the dining room one Sunday morning and we were talking and laughing in

---

79 Popplewell, Sir Oliver. *The Prime Minister and his Mistress.* (Lulu Publishers, Bloomington. USA. 2014) passim

our old accustomed terms. Suddenly, in a single instant, without premonition on my part or any challenge on hers, the scales dropped from my eyes; the familiar features and smile & gestures & words assumed an absolutely new perspective: what had been completely hidden from me was in a flash half revealed, and I dimly felt, hardly knowing, not at all understanding it, that I had come to a turning point in my life."[80]

Asquith had an academic career of very great distinction and a meteoric rise in politics. He was born in 1852. His father died at the age of 35 and Asquith was brought up by an uncle. He went to the City of London School from where he won one of only two classical scholarships to Balliol College, Oxford. It was a remarkable achievement for a boy from a minor public school in competition with other boys, from more distinguished public schools. There he got a first in Mods and was runner up in the Hertford Scholarship. He was twice runner up for the Ireland Prize ("For the promotion of classical learning and taste") and on the second occasion, he was awarded a special consolation prize because of the narrowness of his defeat. Subsequently he was awarded a first in Greats and shared the Craven Scholarship.

He decided to come to the Bar. Here his career suffered a setback. Like many barristers at that time, and since, he had no patronage and, after pupillage, when he was not taken on as a tenant, he, together with two other ex-pupils, set up chambers on their own. It was six years of comparative poverty with few briefs and little prospect. He was able to support himself with writing, teaching, lecturing and marking exam papers. In August, 1877, he married Helen Melland. Asquith described her: "She cared little for society, shrank from every kind of publicity and self-advertisement, hardly knew what ambition meant—a restricting rather than a stimulating influence and knowing myself as I do. I have often wondered that we walked so evenly together"[81].

80 Brock, Michael & Brock Eleanor (eds). *H H Asquith. Letters to Venetia Stanley.* (Oxford University Press, Oxford 1982) p 532
81 Spender, J.A. & Asquith, Cyril. *The Life of Henry Herbert Asquith.* (Hutchinson & Co. London 19320 vol 1 p 73

She died in 1891 and he married Margot Tennant in 1894.Their relationship had started while Helen was still alive.

In 1883, he moved to the chambers of R.S. Wright (later Lord Wright). Here Asquith's legal career started to improve. There were two particular pieces of work which were to prove of importance to his career. He was asked to produce a memorandum for Wright to present to the Attorney General on the theory and practice of the Parliamentary oath. The question arose because Bradlaugh had been elected an MP for Northampton. As a radical atheist, he refused to take the oath. He was not allowed to take his seat. Thereupon the electors re-elected him, to the embarrassment of the Government. The memorandum received the approval of the Attorney General and of the Prime Minister. The second important assignment arose from the introduction of "The Corrupt Practices Act" relating to the conduct of elections, which Asquith helped to draft. To explain the intricacies of the new legislation Asquith, at the invitation of the Attorney, produced a small guide which was published by the Liberal General Assembly. It brought Asquith close to leading figures in the Liberal Party and it also resulted in briefs to appear on behalf of the party in disputed election litigation. In June 1886, he was elected as MP for East Fife.

His legal career took an immense step forward when he was led by Sir Charles Russell QC (later Lord Russell of Killowen) in the Parnell Inquiry. After Russell had destroyed Pigott, the author of the forgeries, evidence was given of how *The Times* had been involved in the publication of the forged letters. Macdonald was one of the principal witnesses called on behalf of *The Times*. Asquith described what happened at the end of Macdonald's examination in chief: "As he (Macdonald) was one of the principal witnesses, it would naturally have fallen to Russell to cross examine him; and I was never more surprised in my life than, when the court rose for lunch, he turned to me and said: "I am tired; you must take charge of this fellow." I protested but in vain and I was left to the critical task of conducting the cross-examination; a task made all the more formidable, because my leader, the greatest cross examiner at the English Bar, sat there throughout and listened. I got on to what proved to be an effective and even, a destructive line of attack, and in the course of a couple of hours, made the largest step in advance that I ever took in my forensic career."[82]

His political career was meteoric. He had been in the House of Commons for only six years. He had made few speeches. He had held no office of any kind and had spent his whole time on the back benches. It came therefore as something of a surprise when, in June 1892, aged not quite forty, Gladstone appointed him to be Home Secretary. Eight of his colleagues were well over sixty and, of the rest, only two were under fifty. Gladstone himself was aged 83. In 1906, the Liberals won an overwhelming majority in the General Election. After some unpleasant intrigue by Asquith, Grey and Haldane to try and persuade Campbell Bannerman, the Prime Minister, to sit in the House of Lords, Asquith found himself as the new Chancellor of the Exchequer. In 1908, after two heart attacks, Campbell Bannerman resigned as Prime Minister to be succeeded by Asquith.

Venetia's relationship with Asquith arose out of a fatal accident suffered in December 1909 by Archie Gordon (son of Lord and Lady Aberdeen). He was Violet's boy friend. Violet and Venetia had been very close friends from their early teens and Venetia had been a frequent visitor to Downing Street. She was ostensibly the daughter of Lord Sheffield, the 4th Baron, who was sometimes known as Lord Stanley of Alderley. She was born in 1887 and lived until 1948. Margot Asquith expressed the view that Venetia was not Lord Sheffield's child. She was believed to have been the daughter of the 9th Earl of Carlisle, with whom her mother had an affair. She and Violet were part of the same social set and used frequently to meet in England, Scotland and France. They wrote gushing girlie letters to each other. In July 1907 Violet wrote: "Goodbye Darling—I wish you weren't gone—write to me very often and don't stop loving me."[83] Venetia replied in much

82 Earl of Oxford and Asquith. *Memories and Reflections* (Cassell and Company ltd. London 1928) pp79-80
83 Bonham Carter, Mark & Pottle, Mark. (Eds) *Lantern Slides. The Diaries and Letters of Violet Bonham Carter.1904-1914.* (Weidenfeld and Nicolson, London 1996) p134

the same vein addressing her as "my Darling" and ending "Goodbye ever dearest". When Archie Gordon was in hospital at Winchester, having been badly injured in a motor accident, Venetia was at his bedside for the last hours with Violet.

The earliest extant letter from Asquith to Venetia is dated 10 September 1910 and thereafter correspondence was spasmodic until 1912. In April 1911, Asquith had gone to the House of Commons complaining of feeling unwell. Margot arranged for a doctor to call and expected Asquith back early. In fact he spent the evening in the Cabinet room writing to Venetia. On 1 April 1912, he wrote to her in these terms: "Dearest Venetia—I want to see you (& must) before you go and I hear from Violet that you might be able to come here (H of C) tomorrow (Tuesday) to hear the Budget; in any case after it, at tea time in my room—you will come won't you?—Ever yr loving, HHA."[84]

At this time, Prime Minister, Asquith was nearly 60 years old. Venetia was aged 24. She had been privately educated by tutors and governesses and it is clear from Asquith's letters that she was an intelligent and well read girl with a good knowledge of English literature and was much interested in politics. Pictures at the time show her dark haired, dark eyed, lively and, though no beauty, not unattractive, although Violet subsequently told Roy Jenkins that: "Venetia was so plain." She has been variously described. "An exciting, brilliant, liberated woman—years ahead of her time. An attractive woman, but far from a stunning one—with intelligence, excitement, force of personality and political sophistication. She was a rebel and a radical, indifferent to convention and always her own person". In the years before the war, she was one of the leading members of a group who came to be known as "The Corrupt Coterie". They held riotous parties. They not only drank too much champagne but also turned to morphine and "chlorers" (chloroform) after dances or death. They flirted outrageously—kissed and sometimes more than that. They evaded chaperones, shocked their parents, whom they sought to outdo in flamboyance, and scandalised society. Diana

---

84 Letters p 19

Cooper wrote: "The Coterie's pride was to be unafraid of words, unshocked by drink and unashamed of decadence and gambling— Unlike—Other-People, I'm afraid. Our peak of unpopularity was certainly 1914 and 1915."[85] They were later described by Asquith as "a rotten social gang –who lead a futile and devastating life."[86]

Whilst Asquith wrote some 560 letters to Venetia of the most passionate sort, and she wrote a large number in reply, her letters are no longer in existence. The relationship has given rise, unsurprisingly, to considerable speculation as to its nature. Some critics contend that this was a platonic friendship, similar to his friendship with other ladies to whom he used to write. Others take a more cynical approach. The view of the Brocks who edited the correspondence between Asquith and Venetia was: "It is almost certain that Asquith never became Venetia's lover in the physical sense and it is unlikely he even wished for it, — not being a love affair in the physical sense, it did not follow any recognisable sequence of passion or satiety."[87] No evidence to support this conclusion is vouchsafed. Roy Jenkins described it: "as an epistolary relationship—which was a solace and relaxation interfering with his duties no more than did Lloyd George's hymn singing or Churchill's late night conversation."[88] Likewise, he provides no evidence for this conclusion.

His views are, in any event, subject to some doubt. When he wrote the revised edition of *Asquith* in 1978, Violet, the stout defender of her father's reputation, was still alive and was allowing Jenkins the use of Asquith's private papers. Although "she did not exactly exercise censorship", it is unlikely that, with his strong liberal democrat credentials, he would wish to write anything likely to antagonise her. Nor did he fully appreciate at the time the full nature and extent of the letters. However, in 1995, he wrote an introduction to Violet's *Diaries and Letters* (*Lantern Slides*). She had died in 1969. He appears to have changed his mind. "The

85 Cooper, Lady Diana. *The Rainbow Comes and Goes*. (Rupert Hart Davis. London 1958) p 82
86 Letters p 607
87 Ibid pp 3 & 13
88 Jenkins, Roy. *Life of Asquith* (Collins, London 1964) p 258

news fifty years later that Venetia exchanged even more frequent and more intimate letters and perhaps other intimacies as well, with Violet's father, was therefore a natural and profound shock, for which I did not allow at the time (i.e. 1978). Compared with today, when the existence of even the most minor and boring scandals is shrieked out from every tabloid, pre-1914 England, was full of hidden sexual reefs."[89]

Diana Cooper has expressed varying opinions. She told the Brocks that Venetia had told her that she, Venetia, was a virgin on her wedding night in July 1915.[90] In May 1915, she had told Duff Cooper that she was quite certain that Venetia was Asquith's mistress and, in February 1984, she told a friend, Angela Lambert, that she believed that the Asquith –Venetia relationship "must have included some sexual contact."[91] Angela Lambert, a friend of both Asquith and Venetia, wrote in her book *Unquiet Souls* that "Asquith had not the temperament for unconsummated love –certainly not platonic love. He was too full blooded to be a Balfour, palely loitering, especially as Margot became disinclined for sex after twenty years of marriage, He was simply an importunate lecher—if he found no resistance to his advances—or even active encouragement—he would take the relationship to its fullest conclusion."[92]

Bates suggests that he was something of a groper. A.J.P. Taylor, after reading the letters, one of which ended "You know how I long for—" observed: "Now what are we to make of that—merely that Asquith wanted to hold Venetia's hand under the carriage rug? I doubt it."[93] In Naomi B. Levine's book, it is said that there were two letters to *The Times*, in which, on the one hand, it was suggested that Venetia told Diana that she had been subjected to a brutal defloration on her wedding night and, on the other, that the writer's father had been Venetia's lover and

---

89 *Lantern Slides.* p xxv
90 Naomi B. Levine. *Politics Religion and Love* (New York University Press.1991.) p 234
91 *Off the Record* p122
92 Lambert p 207
93 Taylor p 25

had been told by her that she had been Asquith's mistress. Unfortunately, neither letter can be found in *The Times* library. Lytton Strachey recalled having been told that "Asquith would take a lady's hand as she sat on the sofa, and make him feel his erected instrument under his trousers."[94] Duff Cooper said of Asquith: "He is oblivious of young men and lecherous to young women."[95]

In the absence of direct evidence that they committed adultery either by way of eye witnesses or admissions, a conclusion about their relationship can only be reached by inference. "The facts of adultery can be inferred from circumstances which by fair inference lead to the necessary conclusion. There must be proof of disposition or inclination and opportunity for committing adultery., but the conjunction of strong inclination and opportunity does not lead to an *irrebuttable* (my italics) presumption that adultery has been committed, nor is the Court bound to infer adultery from opportunity alone."[96] In the instant case there are six particular strands which individually and cumulatively lead to the conclusion that this was indeed an adulterous relationship.

First and foremost is the language and volume of the correspondence. Second, the age and relative status of Asquith and Venetia. Third, the subsequent behaviour of Venetia with a number of married men while still married to Montagu. Fourth, the private communication of highly confidential and secret information, not only before the war but more particularly during the war and his frequent reliance on Venetia's advice on a number of sensitive issues both military and political. The correspondence bears all the hallmarks of sharing a conjugal life. Fifth, in the extensive memoirs of the Asquith family, there is what can only be described as a conspiracy of silence about the very existence of Venetia in Asquith's life. Collectively, the family have simply airbrushed Venetia out of their consciousness. "The dog which didn't bark."

---

94 Holroyd, Michael and Levy, Paul. (eds) *The Shorter Strachey*. (O.U.P.Oxford 1980) pp38-42
95 Ziegler, Philip. *Diana Cooper* (Hamish Hamilton London 1981). P 77
96 *Halsbury Laws of England*. 5th Edition lxx ii para 353

Sixth, there were the frequent arrangements for private meetings which would have provided ample opportunity for lovemaking.

The correspondence started effectively in January 1912 and continued until May 1915. More than 560 are extant. Sometimes they were written once a day, sometimes twice, occasionally three times, and on one occasion four times, the last letter being written at midnight. While some of the letters contain classical allusions, political confidences and references to social events; they are, above all, written in the most passionate and amorous manner. Asquith would often start "my darling", "my dearly beloved", "thank you my darling for your delicious letter" and "most dear." Her frequent letters were described as "delicious" and he made no secret of the fact that he was hopelessly in love with her. Symptomatic of his feelings for her is a letter which he wrote in February 1915: "I am carrying about with me, in my pocket, the most delicious letters you have ever sent me. Nothing for years has given me such intense pleasure as your assurance that you don't want me ever to stop loving you & wanting you. That could never happen."[97] In March 1915, he wrote: "I wonder if you realise how at every hour of the day I am thinking of you" and "In every crisis in my life the thought and love of you dominates everything."[98]

In 1912, Asquith had been Prime Minister for some four years and was aged 62. He had been married twice and had seven children. Venetia was aged 24 and a great friend of Asquith's daughter, Violet who was the same age. The difference in status and age could not be more marked. The subsequent behaviour of Venetia when married may cast some light on her previous behaviour with Asquith. In 1915, she married Edwin Montagu, Asquith's private Secretary, which brought to an end the relationship with Asquith. However, her marriage to Edwin was less than a great success. She had always found him physically unattractive. On one occasion she referred to him "as an old

---

97 Letters p 421
98 Ibid pp 506 & 534

swine."[99] In August 1915, not long after the marriage, Cynthia Asquith found Venetia "in the most extraordinary mood of apparent ennui and lifelessness—I am sure the marooned honeymoon, even if unpleasant, is really the most wholesome. It doesn't do to dodge the situation and each other, by living in a crowd."[100] Raymond Asquith wrote to a friend: "I understand that the terms of the alliance permit a wide licence to both parties to indulge in such extra-conjugal caprices as either may be lucky to conceive."[101]

In May 1918, Diana Cooper wrote in her diary: "Alan Parsons told me that Venetia's letters to Montagu were so unbelievably dreadful that no one, an inch less besotted with love than Edwin, could have tolerated them."[102] In June, she recorded "that Venetia having essentially married him for her days, rather than her nights, was now (after her interval of grass widowhood tortured by real repugnance and that Edwin appeared plunged in gloom."[103] Both Diana and Duff Cooper continued to record that the relations between Venetia and Edwin were getting worse and friends did not feel that there was anything to be done about the marriage "or trying to put the Montagus right, as they don't exist at all."[104]

Given this rather unhappy state of affairs, it is not surprising that Venetia took lovers. The two best known were Beaverbrook and the Earl of Dudley. The liaison with Beaverbrook probably started in 1917 and at the Peace Conference in Paris, in 1919, they were living openly together. Eric Ednam, later the third Earl of Dudley was another lover and was almost certainly the father of Venetia's daughter, Judy, born in February 1923. Among others thought to have been Venetia's lovers, were Lord Charles Hope. Sir Matthew Wilson and Sidney Herbert. One has to ask if

---

99 Asquith Cynthia. p 98
100 Ibid p 74
101 Joliffe, John. *Raymond Asquith. Life and Letters.* (Collins. London 1980) p 202
102 Cooper, Artemis p 57
103 Asquith, Cynthia p 456
104 Ziegler p 75

she was willing to have an adulterous relationship with a number of men when married, why should there be any surprise that she was willing to have an affair with Asquith, a few years earlier, when she was younger and single.

It was not only secret information about vital war secrets that Asquith shared with Venetia, though this was a practice which has attracted the most criticism. Even before the war there were many highly sensitive political problems which Asquith shared with her and on which he sought (and received) her advice. This, he frequently adopted as his own. He thought it important "to have someone from whom he has no secrets, and upon whose understanding judgement and love he can implicitly rely."[105] On another occasion he wrote "I wanted to so much, at the earliest opportunity, and while the impressions are fresh to talk to you & get your opinion about today's War Council."[106] In peacetime, he had sought her opinion about the appointment of new whips, about the appointment of a new Lord Lieutenant in Ireland and of a new Viceroy of India.

In war time, he was telling her about the line of the Allied Armies ("this is quite secret"), losses in the 7th Division ("this is very private"), the bad relations between the French and British generals ("this is very secret") and a number of shipping disasters which he urged her to keep secret. When he told her of the proposal to bombard the Dardenelles, he wrote: "this is supposed to be a secret and indeed I believe it isn't known to some members of the Cabinet—naturally I shall tell you everything—This is all for yourself alone."[107] When in October, it was decided to bomb Cuxhaven he told Venetia, "Nobody knows of this—except W(inston) and myself."[108] He often sent on to Venetia confidential letters or telegrams sent privately to him. As he explained: "I wish we had something like a code that we cd use by telegraph—This morning –I longed to let you know before anyone else, what had

---

105 Letters p 83
106 Ibid p 377
107 Ibid p 423
108 Ibid p215

happened and what was happening."[109] These were the sort of secrets normally shared only between husband and wife.

When the Asquiths came to write their memoirs, biographies and autobiographies it might be expected that Venetia's name would rate some mention, if not a chapter or two. In 1932, J.A. Spender and Asquith's youngest son Cyril (later a Law Lord) wrote the authorised biography of Asquith. It is called *Life of Lord Oxford and Asquith*. It was published in two volumes and runs in all to some 720 pages. There are only two brief references even to the existence of Venetia. The first, in volume one, reads: "He discovered a need for some receptive and sympathetic female intelligence outside the circle of his family, to which he could communicate, as a matter of routine, the spontaneous outflow of thought or humour, of fancy or emotion. A whole succession of women friends responded to this need—Venetia Stanley and latterly Mrs Harrison may be cited as examples." [110] The other mention of Venetia is in a letter he wrote to Margot in 1914 telling her that he played golf at Holyhead with the local professional and Venetia.[111]

The "Chapter of Autobiography" (page 48 ante) in which he movingly describes the occasion in 1912, when he realised the extent of his passion for Venetia, finds no echo in Asquith's *Memories and Reflections*. Published in 1928, in two volumes and running to some 450 pages, they contain no reference to Venetia. In 1926, he had published two volumes of *Fifty Years of Parliament*, consisting of 520 pages, without reference to Venetia. *Letters from Lord Oxford to a Friend*, were published in two volumes in 1933 and 1934. They were letters which he had written to Hilda Harrison over a period of some twelve years. The correspondence amounted to about one letter a month and contained no hint of amorous or passionate expression. The contrast with his letters to Venetia could not be more marked. Margot was no more forthcoming. She portrayed his friendship

109 Ibid p192
110 Spender vol 1 p 217
111 Ibid vol 2 p50

with Venetia as being part of the family friendship with her, while contrasting Asquith's friendship with Hilda Harrison with whom" he developed a lasting affection." Her memoirs were no more informative. .Cynthia Asquith too, violently inked over all references (to Asquith's behaviour) in her diary.[112].

There are two volumes of Violet Bonham Carter's *Diaries and Letters* covering a period from 1904 -1915. The first mention of any relationship between her father and Venetia is in May 1915 when she wrote: " He talked about every sort of politics— Venetia—Margot—Venetia rested him from all this (attacks by the press)," The second entry quotes a letter from Margot and reads "Father is happier over V's marriage-(to Edwin)— he thinks he wd mind less were it anyone else but I tell him whoever she married he wd mind deeply as he has been very much in love—" Given that Violet and Venetia had been intimate friends for some ten years and exchanged intimate letters to each other, it is surprising that Violet makes no reference to any sort of relationship between Venetia and Asquith. Again,"The dog that didn't bark".

The next strand is the opportunity they had for an adulterous relationship. There are constant references to his disappointment when they cannot meet There was a regular arrangement that they would meet on Fridays when they would go out together in Asquith's car. His descriptions of their meetings follow a familiar pattern: "I look back on our delicious time together yesterday and forward to Saturday and Sunday." It was delicious having you last night at dinner though the conditions might have been better"— "solace and joy as the thought of you and our delicious drive "Yes we had a divine time all too short, tho longer than one could have hoped."[113] "Looking back, I can hardly remember a day out of 365 when I have not written to you or seen you or both."[114] He summed up the pleasures of their drives together when he wrote: "I will undertake to say that in the hundred or more of our drives,

---

112 Beauman, Nicola. *Cynthia Asquith*. (Hamish Hamilton.London 1987) p 195
113 Letters pp 50.56,62 & 71
114 Ibid p347

there has been the greatest interchange of "Fun" in the widest sense, than as ever happened in our time, or perhaps my time, between man and any woman. "[115]

There is one final piece of evidence to complete the picture. Asquith had had five children by Helen and five by Margot, three of whom had died at birth. For Margot, pregnancy was a nightmare. Post-natal depression for which there was no alleviation but time, brought on insomnia of which she was afraid. As a result, in 1907, the doctors decided that they must take a firm line "there must be no more children, not the slightest risk must be taken."[116] For Asquith it was to lead to serious consequences. Here was a man aged 55, in the prime of his life, vigorous, virile and (as his contemporaries vouchsafed) attractive to and attracted by young women, who was now to be banished from the marriage bed and confined to sleeping apart from his wife in a separate bedroom. Why then should it occasion any surprise, if within a few years, he should seek solace from a young woman like Venetia, half Margot's age, in order to escape from his celibate life? It is self-evident that she became his mistress. Once again the predator and prey played their allotted parts.

---

115 Ibid p586
116 Bennett p 174

CHAPTER EIGHT

OSCAR WILDE

The story of Oscar Wilde and Lord Alfred Douglas (his lover), the son of the Marquis of Queensbury, illustrates what Parris described, particularly in relation to politicians, as "the vanity and craving for applause and a drive to keep asking for more until something big and external to yourself finally fells you." Thus it was that Wilde's ill-judged action against the Marquis for accusing him of "posing as a somdomite" (sic) resulted in his subsequent downfall and humiliation from which he never recovered. "His completely and persistent unrealistic belief in his own good luck" also played a large part in his decision, after the failure of his action against the Marquis, not to flee the country and avoid arrest.

Wilde was born in October 1854 in Dublin. His father was an ear and eye surgeon and his mother collected paintings and busts of ancient Rome and Greece. In 1871, Wilde won a scholarship to Trinity College, Dublin. He read classics and had an outstanding academic career there, finishing up with the award of the Berkeley Gold Medal, the highest honour in Greek which the University could bestow. From there, with a scholarship, he went to Magdalen College, Oxford where he read Greats. At Oxford, he joined a group of aesthetes, wearing long hair, outrageous clothes and adopting a languid approach to life in which manly sports played no part. His rooms were decorated with blue china, lilies, peacock feathers and sunflowers.

He left Oxford in 1878 having won the Newdigate Prize for a poem and got a double first in Mods and Greats. For the next ten years he earned a living by writing poems, books and plays and giving lectures in London, Paris and America. He also wrote articles on artistic and literary subjects for various magazine. In 1884, he married Constance Lloyd by whom he had two sons. In 1886, Wilde being physically repelled by his wife's pregnancy, was seduced by a 17 year old, attractive, precocious boy called Robert Ross, the son of a distinguished Canadian lawyer,[117] He had come to stay at Tite Street, the Wilde's home, before going up to Cambridge and initiated Wilde in homosexual acts.

In 1891, Wilde, aged 37 met Lord Alfred Douglas, known as "Bosie," then an undergraduate at Oxford aged 20. He was young, handsome and sensuous. He introduced Wilde to young working class male prostitutes known as rent boys. Wilde would meet them, take them out to a private dinner, provide them with gifts and then to a hotel. Bosie became Wilde's constant companion, staying with him in Bad Homburg and at the farm-house rented by the Wilde's in Norfolk. When rehearsals for *A Woman of no Importance* were due to take place they shared rooms at the Savoy but it was the introduction, by Bosie, of the pimp Alfred Taylor, the blackmailer Charlie Parker and of the young rent boys which eventually was to cause Wilde's downfall. The immediate problem for Wilde however was the bitter animosity felt by the Marquis of Queensbury, Bosie's father, about Bosie's relationship with Wilde. Queensbury made a whole series of intemperate threats and insults against Wilde. On one occasion he went to Wilde's house, unannounced and threatened him and, on the first night of *The Importance of Being Earnest*, when the police were called he was refused entry to prevent him disrupting the play.

Sometime later, Queensbury left his card at Wilde's club, the Albermarle, having written "To Oscar Wilde, posing somdomite (sic)".Wilde considered proceedings against Queensbury and sensibly Ross advised against it. However, Bosie insisted and Queensbury was arrested and stood trial. There were some ten boys, who were to be called by Queensbury, whom Wilde was alleged to have solicited to commit sodomy. Edward Carson

---

117 Ellman, Richard, *Oscar Wilde*. (Penguin Books, London.1988) p 259

QC, counsel for Queensbury cross-examined Wilde about his association with young men. Wood, for instance, was an unemployed young clerk who had attempted to blackmail Wilde but before that had been entertained to supper and received £2 as a present. Shelley, an office boy, aged 20, had been taken to dinner by Wilde in a private room at the Albermarle Club with a connecting door to a bedroom where he and Wilde had drunk large quantities of whiskies and soda. He had also had been taken by Wilde to the theatre, to an exhibition and to clubs and cafes. He had been paid on three occasions by Wilde. Conway was a newspaper boy, aged 18, to whom Wilde had given an expensive silver mounted walking stick as well as a brand new serge suit which he wore when he went on an overnight trip to Brighton with Wilde.

Parker was an unemployed valet whom Wilde had lavishly entertained in private rooms at restaurants and clubs in London. Other names suggested were Scarfe, a 20 year old unemployed clerk, Mayor, to whom Wilde had given a silver cigarette case and who had spent the night in Wilde's rooms and 16 year old Grainger, who worked as a servant for Douglas.[118] The threat of some of these youths being called to give evidence persuaded Wilde to drop the prosecution of Queensbury. The same afternoon Wilde was arrested, although Ross advised him earlier to leave at once for France, but he refused. He was then charged with acts of gross indecency with a number of young men. The jury disagreed and a further trial was ordered pending which Wilde was on bail. A second trial ended in a conviction and a sentence of penal servitude in Reading gaol.

Wilde's description of his feelings in *De Profundis* fully supports Parris' view about the effect of the aphrodisiac. Wilde wrote: "People thought it dreadful of me to have entertained at dinner evil things of life and to have found pleasure in their company.—It was like feasting with panthers; the danger was half the excitement. I used to feel like a snake charmer must feel

---

118 Foldy, Michael. *The Trials of Oscar Wilde* (Yale University Press Newhaven and London. 1997) pp 13-17.

when he lures the cobra to stir from the painted cloth or reed basket that holds it and makes it spread its hood at his bidding and sway to and fro in the air as a plants sways restfully in a stream. They were to me the brightest of gilded snakes, their poison was part of their perfection.[119] Desire at the end was a malady, a madness or both I grew careless of the lives of others. I took pleasure where it pleased me and passed on. I forgot that every little action of the common day makes or unmakes character.[120] I wanted to eat of the fruit of all the trees in the garden of the world—And so indeed I went out and so I lived, My only mistake was that I confined myself so exclusively to the trees of what seemed to me the sun-lit side of the garden, and shunned the other side for its gloom."[121]

After Wilde's release, he and Bosie were reunited for a short time in Naples but financial hardship to both resulted in a parting of the ways. Later, Bosie was violently to repudiate Wilde's sentiments and friendship, and to be highly critical of his works. Jealousy of Ross played its part in this and Bosie involved him-self in a number of high profile sensational libel cases which resulted in him also being sent to prison. He died in 1945 nearly half a century after the death of Wilde. In happier days, they had enjoyed a relationship which they both arrogantly believed made them untouchable. Hubris and an exaggerated self belief finally felled them both.

---

119 Wilde, Oscar, *De Profundis*. (Holland Hart –Davis. London 2000) p 130
120 Ibid p 3.
121 Ibid p 739

CHAPTER NINE

HORATIO BOTTOMLEY

Horatio Bottomley was a swindler on a grand scale who used his skills as a confidence trickster to amass large sums of money by fraud. In particular, at an early age he realised the power of the press and through the ownership of a number of magazines, he was able to persuade a gullible public to invest in a large number of bogus schemes. His superb oratorical skills were deployed, not only to persuade investors to part with their money, but also to defeat a whole series of criminal prosecutions arising out of his businesses.

Bottomley was born in March 1860. His early life was spent in an orphanage but at the age of 14 he ran away. Eventually he went to London after working as an errand boy and there, after being apprenticed to a wood engraver, he became an office boy with a firm of solicitors. His mother and uncle were friendly with Charles Bradlaugh, who was a Republican and eventually a highly controversial Member of Parliament. Because he refused to take the Parliamentary oath Bradlaugh was not allowed to take his seat when elected on several occasions, until the government changed the law. He took upon himself the role of a mentor to Bottomley.

After learning shorthand at Pitman's College, Bottomley joined a larger solicitors' firm where he learnt the rudiments of legal procedure. Bradlaugh encouraged Bottomley to read more widely, including the works of Darwin and Huxley. Interest in the law resulted in Bottomley joining Walpole's, a firm of legal shorthand writers and becoming a partner. In 1884, he entered the world of publishing. It was then customary for local debating societies in London, conducted on the same lines as the House of Commons and called Local Parliaments, to flourish. Bottomley had the idea of reporting the proceedings of the Hackney Local Parliament in a paper which he now launched, called the *Hackney Hansard*. The success of this venture encouraged Bottomley to report other Local Parliaments in a weekly publication *The Debater*. In 1885, he founded The Catherine Street Publishing Association. It acquired or produced a number of periodicals and magazines.

They included: *The Municipal Review* (which gave biographical details of local mayors on the understanding that a large number of copies would be ordered for local distribution); *Youth* (a boy's paper); and *The Financial Times* (a rival to *The Financial News*). He needed capital for this project and in 1886 he approached an Irish entrepreneur, called Osborne O'Hagan. He was told by O'Hagan that the business was too small but, if it were a printing business, O'Hagan might be interested. Bottomley found printers called MacRae and O'Hagan formed a Company including The Catherine Publishing Association and Curtis and Company, newspaper publishers. It was now called MacRea, Curtis. Bottomley became chairman. The Company had a capital of £100,000 in one pound shares, half of which was underwritten by O'Hagan. Shares were offered for sale but only 231 were taken up. A year later, surprisingly, the capital was increased by £20,000 and a dividend of 12% was declared. The shares rose to two pounds.

It was not long before MacRae and Bottomley parted company. MacRea took the newspapers leaving Bottomley with the printing works. Bottomley now obtained an option on the printing of Hansard, the official record of proceedings in Parliament. In 1899, he founded the Hansard Publishing Union Ltd. It was to prove a disaster. The Company had a capital of £500,000 and directors of impeccable rectitude. However, the Anglo-Austrian Printing and Publishing Company which was also founded by Bottomley with much the same directors and share capital absorbed the Hansard Union funds.[122] The idea of the

---

122 Symons, Julien. *Horatio Bottomley* (Cresset Press 1955) pp 3-10

Austrian enterprise was to set up a global printing industry for which purpose Bottomley obtained options on thirteen Austrian printing and publishing firms. He persuaded the directors to pay him £75,000 in order to take up the option which they never did. Bottomley received further cheques to some £13.500. No money except the original capital was received, but nevertheless dividends of 15% were paid on the ordinary shares. No statements of accounts or reports were ever produced and the shareholders eventually issued their own statement of accounts. "The company has acquired no business in Vienna, or elsewhere, has no property whatever and its whole capital appears to be lost."

The Hansard Publishing Union itself had been fully subscribed and as a result of further expansion its share capital was doubled. However the new shares were not fully subscribed, the interest due to the corporation which had underwritten the debenture issue was not paid, and it put in a receiver. Bottomley had taken some £100,000 out of the company. In the result, in April 1891, Bottomley filed for bankruptcy.[123] Bottomley had announced non-existent profits of some £40,000. He had repeatedly bought companies for far less than approved by the directors and had pocketed the difference. In the result, in April 1891, Bottomley was made bankrupt. He told the Official Receiver that he had no idea where the money had gone. The Board of Trade brought criminal proceedings for fraud against Bottomley and three of the Directors.[124]

At the trial in the High Court before Mr Justice Hawkins and a jury in January 1893, the prosecution were represented by Sir Charles Russell QC, The Attorney General, and Sir Charles Rigby QC, The Solicitor General, who led Charles Mathews, C.F.Gill and Henry Sutton, all destined to have distinguished legal careers. Bottomley following the example of his mentor, Bradlaugh, decided to represent himself. Half way through the case Charles Russell, one of the greatest crossexaminers at the Bar, was required

---

123 Ibid
124 Hyman, Alan. *Rise and Fall of Horatio Bottomley.* (Littlehampton Book Service Ltd Worthing. Cassell & Co. 1927) pp 31-35

elsewhere and Charles Rigby, wholly inexperienced in criminal trials, was left to argue the Crown's case before a hostile judge. Hawkins was known as "Hanging Hawkins". He had recently passed a sentence of 12 years on another fraudster but in this case he seems to have taken a shine to Bottomley and, when the jury acquitted him, said that he agreed with the verdict.

It was a stunning triumph for Bottomley where his oratory, eloquence and ingenuity had prevailed. Not only did the result provide some protection from future prosecutions but the result gave the impression to potential investors that here was a man who was not only clever but honest with it.[125] He made an arrangement with his creditors and thus avoided the problems of bankruptcy.

He was now involved in promoting Australian gold mining shares. He reconstructed fallen companies and thereby also made a fortune. One historian wrote "A truly amazing success story, the product of reckless audacity, astonishing energy and extreme good fortune."[126] Reconstruction followed a familiar pattern Shareholders who were faced with a situation, where the company in which they had heavily invested and which was now failing, were told that the provision of more money would save the day. They were invited to buy shares in other companies started by Bottomley. Over a period of some ten years, he floated gold mining companies with a nominal value of some £ 25,000,000 which resulted in huge profits for Bottomley. Dividends were often paid out of capital. It was speculation of the worst sort although the schemes managed to flourish for many years.

The essence of his flotations was that a subscription, then a Stock Exchange quotation, would be followed by a price, artificially raised, and by a dividend of 20%. When as was almost inevitable, the value of the stock declined, there would be liquidation or reconstruction. The name "Ponzi" for such schemes had not yet been invented. Pound shares in a gold mine (Howley)

125 Symons, pp 26-36.
126 Morris,A.J.A. *Bottomley, Horatio William* (Oxford Dictionary of National Biography 2011)

which were said to contain £ 4,000,000 worth of gold eventually changed hands at one shilling and sixpence. (7½ p in modern currency).[127] By the beginning of the 20th century, Bottomley had given up gold mines. He had been invited to be the Liberal candidate for South Hackney. In the General Election of 1900 he was defeated by only 280 votes. He also managed to win a libel action against the editor of *The Critic* who wrote that Bottomley's place was at the Old Bailey and not at Westminster. Bottomley conducted his own case before a judge and jury. Much evidence was given about the Australian mines but Bottomley prevailed and was awarded £1000 by way of damages.

In 1902, he bought a failing London evening paper, *The Sun*, but it was not a financial success and in 1904 he sold it. His political career now took off. In the 1906 General Election he was elected as the Liberal member for South Hackney. The Liberal government, led first by Campbell-Bannerman and then by Asquith, was one of the most distinguished administrations this country has known. Bottomley's maiden speech was "greeted in chilling silence by a House that was well aware of his chequered reputation."[128] While he made a number of useful interventions in debates he was little regarded by his fellow members.

In May 1906, he launched a weekly newsmagazine *John Bull*. It was immediately popular and by engaging Joshua Elias, the managing director of the publishers, Odhams Ltd, to handle the printing, Bottomley was able to concentrate on his journalism. It was full of gossip and scandal and Bottomley was not averse to making false allegations against individuals and companies so that they were prepared to pay either directly or by advertising to avoid further adverse publicity. His reluctance to pay bills resulted in numerous bankruptcy petitions. He introduced a co-operative partnership scheme and suggested to its customers that they should deal in their stocks and shares through the *John Bull* Investment Trust. All the familiar Bottomley devices for extracting money from greedy investors were involved.

---

127 Symons p 55-57.
128 Hyman, Alan. *The Rise and Fall of Horatio Bottomley*. (Cassell. London. 1972) p 76

When, in 1906, one of his reconstructed companies, the Joint Stock Trust and Finance Company went into liquidation, Bottomley was again the subject of a prosecution. Although Bottomley was to arrange that the relevant share ledgers should be removed before the Official Receiver could lay his hands on them, it became clear that the Trust had issued ten million shares in excess of its capital. The case was first heard before Aldermen sitting as magistrates at the Guildhall. Because of illness, the Court was presided over by three different magistrates on separate occasions, and Bottomley again defended himself. Although the case was prosecuted by Horace Avory QC and Richard Muir, two of the most formidable criminal lawyers of their time, the loss of vital documents, the confusion of prosecution witnesses, coupled with Bottomley's dominating personality and oratorical skills, resulted in a triumphal acquittal at the close of the prosecution case. The facts of the case could not conceal that there had been fraud on a grand scale, but it did not prevent investors continuing to believe in the reliability of whatever scheme Bottomley chose to flaunt before their unsuspecting eyes. It was a classic example of the financial three card trick performed by a charming professional con artist.

His political career continued despite adverse publicity and he was re-elected in both the general elections in 1910. However a claim by the executors of Robert Master in 1912, resulting from the purchase of shares in one of Bottomley's Trusts, resulted in an award of some £50,000 against Bottomley. He now had massive debts which he could not pay and was forced into bankruptcy which necessarily involved leaving the House of Commons. *John Bull* remained the vehicle which enabled Bottomley to survive and to become a patriotic figure.

He now used his newspaper to promote lotteries and sweepstakes. The most profitable was the *John Bull* Derby Sweep which had to operate in Switzerland to avoid prosecution in England, where it was illegal. Hundreds of thousands of tickets were sold but there were grave suspicions as to where the winning prizes went. One effect of his various competitions, as well as his self portrayal as a man of the people, raised the circulation of

John Bull to 1.5 million.[129] But it was the war in 1914 which gave Bottomley the great opportunity to exercise his native talents as a patriotic rabble rouser.

He quickly appreciated the public's hatred of all things German and also the importance of giving publicity to grievances by members of the armed forces. But it was as a public speaker, addressing some three hundred public meetings, including recruitment rallies, that he received universal acclaim. His personality was described as "depending on his twinkling grey blue eyes, warm humour, the consciously common touch and the apparent deep sincerity—his triumph was personal and magnetic."[130] While some of the recruiting meetings were without payment, he didn't miss the opportunity at other patriotic lecture tours to take a substantial profit from the occasion.

The Government were reluctant to grant him any official status, nevertheless, when some shipworkers were threatening industrial action on the Clyde in April 1915, Lloyd George, the Chancellor of the Exchequer asked Bottomley to address them. He did and the strike was averted.[131] He was sent on morale boosting visits to the Army in France and to the Grand Fleet at Scapa Flow. *John Bull* continued to flourish though not without some unsuccessful libel actions. It was much in demand among the troops. By the end of the war, Bottomley had become one of the best known figures in the country and had also managed to restore something of his reputation.

He now wished to return to Parliament. Somehow he manged to raise the money (and bonds) to secure a discharge from his bankruptcy and standing as an independent, again at South Hackney, he was elected, securing some 80% of the votes. Although he was to take an active part in the House of Commons and to be invited by the Government as "The Soldiers' Friend" to help to pacify some troops, who were in a state of mutiny because

---

129 Messinger, Gary.S. *Patriotism and Propaganda in the First World War* (Manchester University Press 1972) pp 206-207
130 Symons p 175
131 Messinger. pp 209-210

of delays in demobilisation, he now embarked on an enterprise that was to lead to disaster. In 1919, the government issued Victory Bonds at a cost of £5 and Bottomley found a new way easily to acquire a large profit. He started a Victory Bond Club where subscribers could, for the sum of £1, buy a share in the same bonds and also participate in a prize draw. Bottomley used some of the money to buy two newspapers which failed. In 1920, Odhams took control of *John Bull*.

Initially, the launch of his bonds far surpassed expectation even taking into account the trusting nature of the greedy investors and Bottomley's public standing. But it could not last for ever. Writs were issued against Bottomley by dissatisfied investors, articles in various magazines alleging fraud now became common and his attempt to have his old associate Bigland prosecuted ended in Bigland's acquittal. As a result, Bottomley was charged with fraud in relation to the Victory Bond Club. On 28 May 1922, Bottomley was convicted at the Old Bailey and sentenced to seven years penal servitude. His appeal was unsuccessful. After his release he started a new magazine, *John Blunt* but it failed. Public appearances to raise money were unsuccessful. He was made bankrupt in 1930 and, in May 1933, he died, Parris described him as "a shameless liar and a thief."[132] Bottomley fits neatly into Parris' description of the "Aphrodisiac of Power". "A craving for applause, for being a somebody, for being looked up to—a completely and persistently unrealistic belief in your own good luck—an obsessive drive to keep asking for more until something big and external to yourself finally fells you."[133] On 3 June, 1922, *The New Statesman* wrote: "He elevated roguery to an art. He possessed the sort of genius that repeatedly drew our eyes from his victims, and even the moralist could on occasion suspend his moral sense in order to admire a brilliant display of effrontery."[134]

As for the prey, greed and naivety played equal parts in their expensive disillusionment.

---

132 Spectator 11 August 2001 p 31
133 Ibid 21 May 2011
134 *The New Statesman.*

CHAPTER TEN

VISCOUNT GREY OF FALLODON

On 28 June 1914, Archduke Francis Ferdinand, the heir to the Habsburg throne was assassinated at Sarajevo by a Serbian patriot. Austria, encouraged by Kaiser Wilhelm of Germany, issued an ultimatum to the Serbs which they could not, in honour, accept. Austria started military action against Serbia. Russia mobilised in support of Serbia. Germany then also mobilised. This activated the Franco-Russian alliance and France therefore became involved. Britain had a loose military arrangement with the French. It did not involve Britain automatically declaring war on Germany, if the latter went to war with France. The catalyst for Britain's involvement was the ultimatum by Germany to Belgium. Britain was bound by a treaty of 1839 to guarantee the neutrality of Belgium. On 1 August, the Cabinet, after much debate, decided that the invasion of Belgium was a casus belli, but Members of Parliament were anxious to stay out of war and great uncertainty prevailed about Britain's position. On 3 August at 11am, the Cabinet agreed to mobilisation of the Fleet and Army, but no immediate decision was then taken.

That afternoon, at 3pm, Sir Edward Grey (as he then was), the Foreign Secretary, addressed a packed House of Commons, for over an hour, to persuade them that the German ultimatum to Belgium should be rejected and that the treaty obligations to Belgium must, as a matter of national honour, be respected. The effect of his speech was to convince the waverers in the Cabinet and in the House to support the Government. Accordingly, when, on 4 August, Germany invaded Belgium, Britain went to war with Germany, a decision backed by the country, though three pacifist ministers resigned. Grey's speech to the House of Commons was the zenith of a long unbroken period of office. He had carried a country into war, united, and solved the ministerial crisis which arguably no one else could have accomplished.[135] Grey returned to the Foreign Office at 6pm and later, as dusk fell, was looking out of a window with J.A. Spender, editor of the Westminster Gazette. Observing the lamplighter in the Park outside, Grey historically remarked: "The lamps are going out all over Europe. We shall not see them lit in our own lifetime" [136]

Edward Grey was born on 25 April 1862. He became Sir Edward Grey in 1882 when his grandfather died (his father having died in 1874) and was created 1st Viscount Grey of Fallodon in the County of Northumberland in 1916.He was the eldest of six children. His family had political connections; his grandfather, Sir George Grey, had been a Member of Parliament for forty years and was a prominent Liberal politician. He became Home Secretary and held office three times under Russell and Palmerston. One of his ancestors was Earl Grey who, as Prime Minister, in 1832 introduced the Great Reform Bill. Grey's father died of pneumonia aged thirty nine when Grey was only twelve. As a young man, he had had a passion for fishing and shooting. He gained a reputation as a distinguished fly fisherman and in due course he would gain distinction as a famous ornithologist.

His academic career started well enough. He was regarded as clever at Winchester and, in 1880, went up to Balliol to read classics. Midway through his time at Oxford, his grandfather died and Grey was now responsible for a large estate and for the rest of his family He seems not to have done much work at Oxford although he managed a second in Mods. He became University champion at real tennis and won the British championships on five occasions. After switching to jurisprudence, he was sent down in January 1884. The reason was simple. "Sir Edward Grey, having been repeatedly admonished for idleness and having

135 Waterhouse, Michael. *Edwardian Requiem. A Life of Sir Edward Grey.* (Biteback Publishing Ltd, London. 2013) p353
136 Ibid p xvii

shown himself entirely ignorant of the work set him in the vacation as a condition of residence, was sent down—[137] He returned to sit his finals in the summer when he got a third.

Having no particular career in mind, he approached his great uncle, Lord Northbrook, then First Lord of the Admiralty, to find him some serious, but unpaid, employment. In due course, Grey first became private secretary to Sir Evelyn Baring, then British Consul General in Egypt and subsequently unpaid assistant private secretary to Hugh Childers, the Chancellor of the Exchequer. Grey's interest in politics, as well as in economics, literature and poetry had been nurtured by his tutor and mentor at Balliol, Mandell Creighton, a charismatic churchman of striking presence.[138] In July 1884, a Government proposal to extend the franchise to counties on the same terms as had been given to boroughs, was rejected by the House of Lords. A demonstration was organised at Alnwick near where Grey lived and he was invited to speak. As a result, coached by Creighton in public speaking, Grey was encouraged to stand as Liberal candidate at Berwick. In November 1885, at the age of 23 he was elected a Member of Parliament. For thirty years, he remained their MP. In 1892, he was appointed Under Secretary of State for Foreign Affairs.

In the middle of the election campaign in 1885, he had married Dorothy Widdrington. They had met when out hunting at Christmas and by July they were engaged. In October, they were married. She quickly acquired Grey's interest in fishing and politics. He described it in this way: "Through our married life I had been in the habit of discussing public affairs and sharing all thoughts with my wife—Her interests and outlook on life were wide and her opinion—was always fresh and independent, sometimes so original as to penetrate new aspects and throw new light on the subject; never was it commonplace or second hand;

---

137 Robbins, Keith *Sir Edward Grey*(Cassell, London 1971) p 16
138 Waterhouse p11

never the outcome of conventional or party or class thought."[139] There is no doubt that Grey was in love with her but unfortunately she disliked the idea of having children and had an aversion to the physical side of marriage. He suggested that they should live as brother and sister.[140] One author wrote "Society had never been able to comprehend Dorothy since she had deliberately given it little chance. She was a solitary, sickly person. The great world meant nothing to her. Her books, few close friends and the quietness of the country were her pleasures. In public she seemed nervous and brittle."[141]

According to an article written in the Journal of Liberal History by Hans Joachim-Heller, Grey had been having an affair with Florence Slee from1892. As a result Florence gave birth to a daughter, Winifred. The author had worked at the Foreign Office under Grey and was Winifred's son. According to the article, when it was clear that Florence was pregnant, an elaborate plot was hatched to conceal the fact of the illegitimate birth and the related scandal. Two German employees of the Slee family arranged for Florence to be taken to Germany. After the birth, Florence returned to England while Winifred lived the rest of her life in Germany. At some time, Florence went through a secret invalid marriage with Grey's younger brother Charles, who was about to leave for Africa. Winifred was known as Winifred Grey and the Grey family provided funds for Winifred. Material collected by Heller gives strong support to the story that Edward Grey was Winifred's father.[142] There may have been other lovers. Grey was a good looking young man, attractive and sociable and on his own in London for long periods of time. But about his relationship with Pamela Tennant there can be no doubt.

She was born in 1871 and was one of the three famous Wyndham sisters, granddaughters of Lord Leaconfield, immortalised

---

139 Grey, Edward. *Twenty Five Years*. (Hodder and Stoughton, London. 1925) p 156
140 Lowndes, Mrs Belloc. *A Passing World* (Macmillan , London 1948) p174-175
141 Robbins p153
142 Waterhouse pp 44-47

in the Singer Sargent painting "The Three Graces". She married Edward Tennant, whose family had made their fortune from the manufacture of chemical dyes in Glasgow. It was a marriage of convenience. She was said to have Royal French blood. At the time of her marriage, she had been in love with Harry Cust, a member of the Souls, Editor of the Pall Mall Gazette and a Liberal MP. A brilliant career forecast for him, came to nothing through drink and womanising. He was forced to marry Nina Welby-Gregory, on her alleging she was pregnant. She was not. Asquith described the marriage to Venetia: "Their union was a hopeless experiment from the first; as you say in your letter today "a tremendous argument against marriage."[143] Cust was something of a serial womaniser and is best remembered as being the father of Lady Diana Cooper, whose mother was the Duchess of Rutland. His love letters to Pamela have survived and he wrote that he dreamt of her "insistently" (sic) and he wanted her back. He loved Pamela more than any of the others. He used to call her "my darling little Pamela."[144] "Everyone was in love with Pamela but she never recovered from the first one—she had a crisis of nerves,"[145]

Unsurprisingly, Pamela's marriage to Edward was unhappy. She was aristocratic and a member of the Souls, with a passion for art and literature as well for the pleasures of the countryside. The writer, Emma Tennant, Pamela's granddaughter, wrote: "the most striking feature of women's genealogy of the Tennants is beauty. Pamela embodied its style at the beginning of the century and was regarded by her contemporaries as a mixture "between a whore of Babylon and the Madonna."[146] Pamela was much given to the occult and the sad death of her son Edward (known as Bim) and daughter Hester in 1916, did nothing to discourage that enthusiasm.

---

143 Letters p 301
144 Tennant, Emma. *Strangers*.(Viking London.1999.) p 123
145 Ibid p 122
146 Ibid pp121& 126

Grey's marriage to Dorothy, because of her attitude, lacked a physical side and it would have caused no surprise that a young, active good looking man in the full bloom of life were to seek solace elsewhere. It was not only her attitude to sex which caused Grey such anguish. It was her attitude to life outside which bordered on the edge of balance. A letter she had written to Grey in 1893 gives a glimpse of her inhibitions. "Where there is so much which is unworthy, how can we remain pure? If our life outside politics was to be muddy and doubtful, the contrast would not be so great, every bit of purity in us, every little bit of heaven shared, is one more shadow cast on the blackness of town life, with its unworthy aims, mistakes and general devilishness." She was to add: "All human relations are a mockery it seems to me".[147] While Grey remained friendly with Tennant, there is little doubt that by 1903, he and Pamela were in love and having an affair. In 1902, Pamela had given birth to a fourth child, David. There is a strong suggestion that Grey was the father.[148]

On 4 February 1906, Dorothy had an accident, when she was thrown from her dog cart and died. She was variously described as "enigmatic, unsympathetic, reserved, self-centred and severe". But that Grey grieved for her loss and cherished her memory is borne out by many letters he wrote and by his memoirs. But equally the excitement of the new Liberal Government and his burgeoning friendship with Pamela did much to soften the blow. Grey, Pamela and Tennant maintained a discreet relationship. Grey was a constant visitor to the Tennants, both in Scotland where they had their family home and at Queen Anne's Gate, within a few minutes walk from the Foreign Office. The Tennants also had a country house, Wilsford Manor, in Wiltshire. In 1921, after Tennant's death in 1920, Grey wrote: "for some period, as I supposed people knew, I have had a very delightful and intimate friendship with Pamela—It did not impair my close relationship with her husband and I was equally in the confidence of them both." He asked her to marry him which they did in June 1922.

---

147 Robbins p 45
148 Waterhouse pp 94-95

That their relationship was no secret is shown by various references in many memoirs.[149] Political colleagues were also well aware. On 20 September 1914, Asquith wrote to Venetia: "Edward Grey came to see me to talk over the military situation. He is in better spirits than he was, and Margot elicited from him at tea time that our Pamela was arriving, to take her usual part in his weekly rest cure"[150] On 9 October 1914, he wrote again: "Grey and Winston dined here last night; it is impossible to find a greater contrast. Pamela who sat next to me, kept a watchful eye on E.G. I am afraid she is rather losing her look of distinction,"[151] On 29 November 1914, he wrote again "–meanwhile E.Grey is taking a Sunday off—he left on Friday, I need not say, for Wilsford."[152] Emma wrote: "Edward Grey who will stand for a time unseen at the door and regard her with helpless admiration—his eyes already soft at the sight of Pamela. Eddy knows, without of course it ever being mentioned, that his wife will marry Grey and live there (Fallodon, Grey's home in Northumberland), should anything happen to him. He and the other Edward (Grey) are already seen as Pamela's two husbands; sometimes he thinks it wouldn't matter at all if he simply slipped away." [153] Pamela and Grey tried for children, but Pamela miscarried when she was on the way to a political meeting. In 1928, at the age of 57, she died.

The three most prominent Liberals, when the Conservative Government fell in 1905, were Asquith, Haldane and Grey, with Campbell-Bannerman as the leader. It was thought that the latter would be no match at the dispatch box when faced by Balfour, the Conservative leader. An intrigue then took place to persuade Campbell Bannerman to go to the Lords. In effect, they held a pistol at his head threatening not to serve under him if he remained in the Commons. The three met in Scotland at Grey's fishing lodge at Relugas. There they agreed what became known as the "Relugas Compact." Campbell-Bannerman would go to the Lords, Asquith

---

149 Sc Mrs Belloc Lowndes, Angela Lambert, Emma Tennant, & Waterhouse.
150 Robbins p 214
151 Ibid p 269
152 Ibid p324
153 *Strangers* p 60

was to be the leader of the Commons and Chancellor of the Exchequer, Grey was to be Foreign Secretary and Haldane, Lord Chancellor. However, notwithstanding pressure from the King, Campbell-Bannerman refused to go to the Lords. Eventually Haldane agreed to go to the War Office and Grey and Asquith took office under Campbell-Bannerman, until the latter resigned in 1908.

One of Grey's first policy decisions was to enter into an agreement with the Russians with the idea of maintaining a balance of power in Europe together with France as a counter-weight to the threat of Germany, about which Grey had been anxious for a number of years. The Anglo-Russian Entente in 1907 was the result. Attempts by Germany to expand their interests n the Mediterranean, including the despatch of the gunboat "Panther" to Agadir, merely served to increase Grey's determination to protect the Entente Cordiale with France. The outbreak of war in August 1914 meant that foreign policy was subordinate to the exigencies of the military situation though Grey was instrumental in negotiating secret treaties with neutrals, which was to cause some embarrassment when they came to light at the war's end. When Asquith ceased to be Prime Minister in 1916, and was replaced by Lloyd George, Grey went into opposition and went to the House of Lords as Viscount Grey of Fallodon. In 1919, he became Ambassador to the United States until 1920, but, because of recurring blindness, he gradually withdrew from politics. In 1928 he became Chancellor of Oxford University.

After he died in 1933, there were a number of highly critical comments about his abilities. Chief of these were contained in Lloyd George's "War Memoirs" published in 1938. "He was a calamitous Foreign Secretary, both before and during the War." In talking of charlatans and skunks, Lloyd George wrote "Grey certainly belongs in the first category."[154] Lloyd George's venom against his former Liberal colleagues even 20 years later, explains

---

154 Lloyd George, David, *War Memoirs*, (Little, Brown And Co. Boston.USA. 1937) p 111

why the great Liberal Party of 1906 fell into obscurity in the years after 1918 and which continues to the present day. Ramsay MacDonald said: "I believe him to have been the most incompetent Foreign Secretary—and one of the most honest men who ever held office—one who combined a most admirable intention with a tragic incapacity to drive his way to his own goal."[155] But his name will ever be linked to one of the greatest administrations this country has ever known. He enabled the country to enter the First World War united. The love affair between him and Pamela made no distinction between prey and predator.

---

155 Robbins p 370

CHAPTER ELEVEN

LLOYD GEORGE AND FRANCES STEVENSON

David Lloyd George was born in Manchester on 17 January 1863. In 1911, he met Frances Stevenson, who was teaching at a girl's boarding school at Allenswood, in Wimbledon. His eldest daughter Mair died in 1907 at the age of eight. She had been at school with Frances. In 1911, Lloyd George asked Frances if she would come to Criccieth in Wales and coach his youngest daughter, Megan, who subsequently became Megan Lloyd George MP. Frances stayed during the summer. The coaching continued into the winter. In the summer of 1912, she again went to Criccieth. They fell in love. She gave up teaching and became one of Lloyd George's secretaries at the Treasury. "on his own terms, which were in direct conflict with my essentially Victorian upbringing."[156] He was at this time Chancellor of the Exchequer and one of the most important members of a distinguished Liberal government.

In her diary entry for 21 January 1915 she wrote "It is just two years since C (her private name for him as Chancellor) and I were "married" and our love seems to increase rather than diminish. (He was 50 and she was not yet 25). He says I have taken the place somewhat of Mair," my little girl whom I lost" as he always calls her. He says I remind him of her & make up a little for the loss."[157] He had started writing love letters to her in the

---

156 Lloyd George, Frances. *The Years that are past.*(Hutchinson & Co Ltd. London 1967.) p 53
157 Ibid p 23

autumn of 1912 as her diary entries make clear. "C said this morning he wished I had kept the love letters he wrote two years ago "[158]

In early 1915, Frances had a row with her parents with whom she was living, about her relationship with Lloyd George. His wife and family were safely tucked away in Wales and she came to live in the house at Walton Heath, where Sarah Jones, Lloyd George's faithful retainer looked after her. It had been a gift to Lloyd George from Sir George Riddell. Thereafter their correspondence continued for some thirty years. On 23 October 1943, they were legally married at Guilford Registry Office. On 26 March 1945, Lloyd George died. Frances herself survived until December 1952.

Shortly after Lloyd George's birth, his father gave up being a schoolmaster and moved to Pembrokeshire, in Wales. In 1864 he died when Lloyd George was seventeen months old. The family moved to North Wales and they lived at Llanystumdwy. There, Lloyd George was brought up by his uncle, Richard Lloyd (or Uncle Lloyd as was always called). Uncle Lloyd belonged to a Baptist sect of stern simplicity and was an unpaid minister for some sixty years He was a master craftsman and a great reader of books. He had a passionate interest in Welsh affairs and imbued in the young Lloyd George a desire to further the cause of Welsh Nationalism. He was thus able to subsume his ambitions in the success of his nephew. Uncle Lloyd encouraged Lloyd George to read books and they discussed politics, and subsequently he took an active part in advising him to seek his future as politician. But first there was schooling. Lloyd George started at the age of four at the local village school. He was promoted from the infant class at the age of seven, jumping a class and at twelve he had reached the highest standard in elementary schools. He was also an early reader of Euclid, sometimes while seated in the top branches of an oak tree. While he was a slow reader, he was a very quick learner and whatever he learnt, he was able to retain because he had

---

158 Ibid p 3

the ability to concentrate, he had a tenacious memory, and an independence of mind.[159]

After leaving school, he sat the Law preliminary exam at Liverpool in 1877 at the age of fourteen. This required a knowledge of both Latin and French. He had learnt the former at school. The latter he picked up at home with Uncle Lloyd as his tutor. After passing the exam in 1878, he started work with a firm of solicitors at Portmadoc, called Breese, Jones, and Casson. In 1879 he was articled to Casson. He stayed with the firm for four years passing his intermediate exams in 1881 and his finals in 1884. When the family moved to Criccieth, he went to live there and it became his family home. He was not offered a partnership with the firm and turned down the offer to be a managing clerk at their Dolgelly office. He bravely set up office on his own, working initially from home and eventually opening an office in Portmadoc and subsequently at Pwhelli, Criccieth and Ffestiniog. There his brother William and he practised under the name of Lloyd George and George.

His first political involvement arose when he was an articled clerk. He was asked by Breese, the local Liberal agent, to help with canvassing and with registration. Thereafter, he spoke regularly in public debates at Portmadoc and Criccieth and was widely praised in a variety of local papers. But it was in 1889 that he was involved in a piece of litigation which was to have a profound effect on his legal practice and, more importantly, on his future political career. Lloyd George was passionate in his belief in Welsh Nonconformity as well as being a fierce champion of Welsh tenant farmers. The litigation concerned the rights of burial at the church at Llanfrothen. In 1864, Mr and Mrs Owen had given a piece of land to the church. In 1880 Parliament had passed an Act (The Osborne Morgan Burial Act) which allowed Nonconformists to be buried in accordance with their own rites in parish churchyards. Nonconformists began to use the Owen land. The rector objected and persuaded Mrs Owen to amend the conveyance

---

159 Grigg, John. *The Young Lloyd George.*(Eyre Methuen Ltd .London 1973) p 33

to contain a provision that only Anglican rites could be used at burials, on the piece of land she had given.

In 1888 an old quarryman died and wished to be buried next to his daughter according to Nonconformist rites. The Rector refused and locked the gate. The family advised by Lloyd George, broke into the churchyard and buried the quarryman beside his daughter, according to their own rites. The Rector sued the family. At the County Court, the jury ruled in the family's favour on the ground that the original Owen conveyance came within the provisions of the Osborne Morgan Burial Act and that the subsequent conveyance by Mrs Owen, with its amendment, was invalid. The judge however, after two months delay, gave a verdict in favour of the rector. By mistake he failed properly to record the findings of the jury and, when the matter came before the Court of Appeal, presided over by the Lord Chief Justice, the jury's verdict was upheld and Lloyd George's clients were awarded their costs.

On 24 January 1888, he married Margaret Owen (no relation of the owner of the Church land) whom he had been courting for some eighteen months. There were problems about their getting married. Her family were Methodists and his were Baptists. There were also differences of political allegiance. Her family were also worried about his future financial prospects. Eventually they resolved their differences. After the marriage, they tended to lead separate lives. She was happier looking after her children and garden at Criccieth while he found that he was very much on parade while he was there and so set up home in London. In March 1890, the sitting Conservative MP for the Caernavon Boroughs, Edmund Swetenham Q.C. died. A by-election took place. Lloyd George won by the narrow margin of eighteen votes.

Lloyd George's early efforts in Parliament were devoted to Welsh affairs but in 1897, his political career was affected by allegations of adultery with a Mrs Edwards and a Mrs Tim Davies. Relations between him and Margaret had started to fracture, with his spending more and more time in London and her in Criccieth. She wrote "This business, (Mrs Tim) I tell you, comes between you and me, more so than you can imagine and is growing, and you know it and yet you cannot shake it off. It pains me to the quick and I am very unhappy. If you must go on, I don't know where it will end—beware don't give place for any scandal."—[160] He replied "You threaten me with a public scandal. Alright expose me if that suits you—but you will not alter my resolution to have neither correspondence nor communication of any sort with you until it is more clearly understood how you propose to guide your course for the future. I have borne it for years and have suffered in health, and character. I'll stand it no longer, come what may". He finished one letter, by threatening that if she made him miserable, he would find consolation elsewhere.[161] His relations with Mrs Tim continued for a long while. Frances was much more tolerant as appears from her diaries "I think he is very kind and nice to her and I would not have it otherwise."[162] "He always tells me when he is going (to have tea with Mrs Tim) so I don't mind so much."

Mrs Edwards' involvement with Lloyd George was rather more mysterious. Mrs Edwards was married to a Dr Edwards. They had ceased to have intercourse some two years before 1896. A child was born to Mrs Edwards on 19 August 1896. She made a confession that that was a result of intercourse with Lloyd George on 4 February 1896 and that they had had intercourse on other occasions. Lloyd George had in fact stayed at the Edwards' house on the night of 4 February. The legal proceedings which followed were bizarre. Mrs Edwards alleged cruelty against her husband including the allegation that he had forced her to sign the confession. Dr Edwards then alleged adultery by his wife, not with Lloyd George but with a station master called Edward Wilson. Lloyd George denied any adultery with Mrs Edwards and was not made a co-respondent. At a hearing on 18 November, Mrs Edwards withdrew her cruelty allegations and admitted adultery with an unknown person but not with Wilson. Wilson elected to give evidence and was exonerated. Lloyd George could have given

---

160 Earl Lloyd George Collection. National Library of Wales. p 241
161 Ibid pp 241-243
162 Diary. April 15, 1915. p 46

evidence but on his brother's advice did not do so. This was good advice and had none of the consequences which resulted from Sir Charles Dilke taking the same course.

Allegations of infidelity pursued him throughout his life. Not for nothing was he called the Welsh Goat. In July 1909, *The Bystander* published an article headed "INDISCRETIONS –IRISH AND OTHERWISE" which read "All is not going well with Mr Lloyd George in his new and exalted sphere. Not only is he having a most uncomfortable time politically—but rumour is now busy as to the existence of another kind, which is even less likely to prove of assistance to his career. Mr Lloyd George, has, of course, been overloaded with flattery of late, especially from the fair sex, which is always difficult for a man of "Temperament" to resist. The matter may of course be kept quiet. Alas, it may not. Nous verrons." Six weeks later the Bystander published a grovelling apology and paid damages to the Caernarvon Cottage Hospital. But further allegations continued. The People published a series of articles suggesting that Lloyd George was about to be named as co-respondent, that he was plainly guilty but that attempts to compromise the case had been successful. Again Lloyd George sued and this time he gave evidence. The paper offered no defence and paid substantial damages.[163] Frances had no great belief in his fidelity. In 1929 she wrote: "I promise to be good, & I only hope you are keeping your promise, too. I know you will say there are no opportunities but I don't trust you not to get into mischief anywhere!"[164]

Given the frequency of the allegations of his indiscretions, it is perhaps very surprising that his liaison with Frances was not more the subject of public knowledge or criticism. His political career continued successfully but his opposition to the Boer War, which started in 1899, resulted in enormous unpopularity for him. Opposition to his views showed itself in rowdiness and violence at his meetings which came to a head in December 1901 he went to

---

163 Owen, Frank. *Tempestuous Journey.*(Hutchinson & Co (Publishers) Ltd London 1954.) pp 162-163
164 *My Darling Pussy* p 115

the Birmingham Town Hall for a Liberal Association meeting. There was a crowd estimated at 30,000 who were armed with an assortment of lethal weapons. They succeeded in overpowering the police and entering the hall. Lloyd George managed no more than a few words when the platform was rushed and he escaped by the skin of his teeth, smuggled out by the police and disguised as one of them.

In 1905, the Conservative Government fell and the Liberals under Campbell-Bannerman took office. It was by any standard one of the great administrations in English political history in which Lloyd George played a leading role. In December 1905, he became President of the Board of Trade with a seat in the Cabinet. When the House of Lords rejected the Liberal Education Bill, Lloyd George issued a warning which became a clarion call to his supporters —"if the House of Lords persists in its present policy—it will come on an issue of whether this country is to be governed by King and Peers or by the King and his People."[165] The mantra was to be repeated over the next few years in conflicts over the budget and social legislation.

In 1908, Campbell-Bannerman resigned and Asquith succeeded him as Prime Minister. But, for Lloyd George personally, the emergence of the Marconi scandal occupied his political life from April 1912 until June 1913. Briefly, the English Marconi Company was to set up a chain of wireless stations under a government contract. The Managing Director was Godfrey Isaacs, brother of the Attorney General, Rufus Isaacs. There was an American Marconi Company in which the British Company held more than half the shares. When the American Company was reconstructed there was a large issue of new shares and Lloyd George, at the suggestion of Rufus Isaacs, bought about 2,500 shares. When the Government announced the contract with the British Marconi Company and it was clear that Government ministers were involved in buying shares, there was a public outcry, leading to a Committee of Inquiry. This proceeded, on party lines, to acquit the Ministers of impropriety. The

---

165 *Tempestuous Journey.* p149

Conservative members however, criticised the Ministers for their behaviour. Although Lloyd George appeared to be exonerated, the fallout from the scandal endured for his lifetime.

Thereafter he became successively Minister of Munitions, Minister of War and, in 1916, Prime Minister. He fought the General Election in 1919 and won but his coalition with the Conservatives came to an end in October 1922. Lloyd George's reputation suffered, not only from the Marconi scandal, but also from his involvement in the sale of political honours. This was for his own private benefit and for that of his political chest, particularly from those with close connections to newspapers. Eventually legislation to prevent repetition of the sale of honours was introduced and Maundy Gregory, who was the principal agent in these transactions, was finally prosecuted and convicted.

Frances' mother had an Italian father and a French mother but "was more typically Italian than French" and while her Mother was complex and mercurial, the keynote of her father's character was simplicity".[166] He was secretary to a firm of French import agents. Frances had two sisters and a brother. She was interested in books from an early age. At fifteen she was sent to Clapham High School but not before winning a travelling scholarship to go to France. In the fifth form, at the school, she became friendly with Lloyd George's eldest daughter, Mair. She was anxious to go to Cambridge to read classics at Girton or Newnham but was persuaded by a teacher to sit a scholarship to London University. This she obtained and, in October 1907, she went to the Royal Holloway College where she read classics. In November, she learnt of the death of Mair.

After three years she got a degree and a teaching post at a girl's boarding school, Allenswood at Wimbledon. It was while she had this post that on the last Saturday in June 1911, she went to a service at the Welsh Baptist Chapel in Castle Street off Oxford Circus. It was the custom of Lloyd George on that day to attend and address the congregation. "There for the first time I came into contact with the Welsh Chancellor of the Exchequer and instantly

---

166 Ibid p 12

fell under the sway of his electric personality—I felt myself in some mysterious way drawn into the orbit of his influence—my feelings were aroused to something beyond satisfied curiosity."[167]

It so happened that at this time Lloyd George was very concerned that Megan, his youngest daughter, was not being properly educated, and that she needed a good deal of coaching. Frances was suggested as a suitable coach and, in July 1911, she went for an interview with Lloyd George. She described it in this way: "(he) had a magnetism which made my heart leap and swept aside my judgement, producing an excitement which seemed to permeate my whole being. I was strung to the utmost point of awareness by this strange encounter, which meant so much for me, then and forever after.—I was enslaved for the rest of my life—." The summer of 1911 was of perpetual sunshine, sea, sun and mountains, picnics, walks excursions and not least music, hymns and songs".[168] By this time, she and Lloyd George were frequently writing letters to each other and, in the summer, she was offered the post of his secretary. Lloyd George was well aware of the problems of having a mistress and he referred to the story of Parnell and Kitty O'Shea. Parnell had been the leader of the Irish Party and was a considerable political figure. The affair with Kitty O'Shea had the effect of destroying Parnell's career and also the future of the Irish party which was to have disastrous consequences for the long term future of Ireland.

Lloyd George told Frances that "no man has a right to imperil his political party and its objective for the sake of a woman—which meant that no divorce was possible, and that I must not hope for marriage unless and until he could make me his legal wife; with the corollary that if he ever could, he would do so."[169] Lloyd George's letters to Frances were effusive. He used a variety of terms: "My own sweet Pussy," "My own sweet child", "Ma cherie"," My own sweet cariad". Her letters to him were no less passionate. In July 1919 she wrote: "It frightens me, now, cariad,

167 Ibid p 40
168 Ibid pp 42,43 &47
169 Ibid p 52

when I realise how you are all in all to me, & how nothing in the world matters to me but you. Is it not a terrible thing to have staked your all like that, on one person? It would be, but I know that person is mine, & that he will not fail me, & that I can lean on him & trust in him, & that he is my father & lover & friend. You are all that to me, my beloved, and much more, and a thousand times over, & oh! I love you so.! I kiss you a hundred thousand times. Pussy."

Lloyd George's anxiety not to follow the example of the tragedy of Parnell was surprisingly well achieved. That, for some thirty years, as one of the two most famous politicians in the country, he was able to pursue a liaison with Frances without a public scandal or public condemnation is quite remarkable. In a modern world with media attention at its most feverish, it is unlikely that the result would be the same today. Lloyd George's reputation was affected by the Marconi scandal and by the sale of honours but his continuous election for several decades as an MP speaks volumes for the successful concealment of his adultery with Frances. He had influential friends in the Newspaper world which no doubt contributed to the Press' silence. When Lloyd George died in October 1943, *The Times* naturally published a whole page obituary. Frances was mentioned only once, as having married Lloyd George in 1943 and as" having been his private secretary since 1913."[170] (One might say in modern parlance – economical with the truth.) What is clear in their case, is that the relationship between predator and prey enured to their mutual benefit and had no political fallout.

---

170 *The Times*. 27 October 1943. p 2

CHAPTER TWELVE

THE HARMSWORTHS

Alfred Harmsworth, later Viscount Northcliffe, seduced Louisa Smith, the family servant from Essex, when he was in his teens. She bore him a son. He subsequently had a long time mistress, a Mrs Wrohan, who bore him two sons and a daughter. But it was not a sexual power that he and his brother, Harold, later Lord Rothermere, sought to exercise. As newspaper proprietors their self-inflated ego caused them to imagine that the power which they had, could be used to run governments, dictate policy and decide matters of state. It therefore came as a considerable shock when, at the height of their powers, each of them was separately humiliated in the most public way, Northcliffe by Lloyd George and Rothermere by Baldwin.

Alfred was born in Ireland in 1865 but was brought up in England. He started his career in publishing at school, and later contributed to a number of periodicals. He edited *The Bicycling News* and when he launched *Answers*, his career took off. Thereafter, he published a number of periodicals including *Comic Cuts* and, for women, *Forget-me-not*. His first venture into tabloid newspapers was to buy *The Evening News* in 1894 and then to merge two Edinburgh papers to form *The Edinburgh Daily Record*. Subsequently he published *The Daily Mail*, once famously described by Lord Salisbury as "written by office boys for office boys". He turned *The Weekly Dispatch* into what became the highly successful *Sunday Dispatch*. In 1903, he founded *The Daily Mirror*, in 1905, he acquired *The Observer*, and in 1908, both *The Times*, and *The Sunday Times*. Unsurprisingly, he took an active part in criticising politicians and their policies. His own attempts to enter politics as a Conservative candidate at Portsmouth in 1895, had proved unsuccessful and he decided not to try again. Something of his ambition can be judged from his comment (He was just 30) "My place is in the House of Lords where they don't fight elections."[171] In 1905, he achieved this ambition, being created Baron Northcliffe.

He was a fierce opponent of Lloyd George's budget and the Liberal attempt to reduce the powers of the House of Lords. He did not support the Suffragette movement. When the war started in 1914, his papers took on the s responsibility of dictating to Asquith's Liberal Government how the war needed to be run. The British Expeditionary Force had been engaged in bitter fighting at the Battle of Mons and, in supporting the French retreat, had suffered casualties. On August 30 1914, *The Times'* correspondent, Arthur Moore wrote a sensational article about a "broken army" and "broken bits of many regiments" which caused great offence to the Army. It earned the paper a severe rebuke in the House of Commons from Asquith and a letter of condemnation from Churchill, now First Lord of the Admiralty.

Northcliffe was again at odds with the Government over the "Shell Scandal", a complaint that the Army was being handicapped by the lack of munitions. It resulted, with Northcliffe's vociferous support, in the appointment of Lloyd George as Minister of Munitions in 1915. Intrigue by Northcliffe also resulted in the forcing of a coalition government, with Tories joining the Liberals. Asquith was well aware of Northcliffe's intriguing. He wrote to Venetia Stanley: "There is, in the Tory Press, a dead set being made against me personally. Witness the articles in *The Times* & *The Morning Post*. As you know I am fairly indifferent to press criticism. The idea is that Northcliffe (for some unknown reason) has been engineering a campaign to supplant me"[172] But it was a violent attack on Lord Kitchener, who had retained the post of War Minister in the Coalition Government, which resulted in widespread public anger and condemnation. Copies of *The Daily*

171 Lee Thompson, J. *Northcliffe* (John Murray Publishers. Ltd 2000) p 30.
172 Letters p 517

Mail were burnt in the City of London and advertising and circulation were drastically reduced.

One other vitriolic attack was more successful. Haldane had been one of the leading figures in the Liberal party. He was a man of formidable intellect. He had been responsible for the modernisation of the Army as Minister of War until 1912, when he became Lord Chancellor. Being a scholar of great distinction he had intellectual ties with Germany. This was enough for Northcliffe to pillory him in his papers as pro-German, citing Haldane's description of his college days in Germany "as his spiritual home." The spiteful campaign to get rid of Haldane from the Government was successful. It was left to Haig to restore Haldane's reputation. As the victorious Commander of the British Army in France, Haig made it his business to call on Haldane after the Peace Parade in London in April 1919. There he was to present Haldane with a copy of his War Despatches. Haig inscribed them: "To the greatest Secretary of State for War, England has ever had."

This was not the only attack on military figures which Northcliffe and Rothermere launched during the war. Haig and Robertson (Chief of the General Staff) were the subject of constant abuse and criticisms and their tactics ridiculed. The overweening confidence of the newspaper proprietors led them to believe that they had only to express a view for it instantly to be adopted as government policy. When Lloyd George became Prime Minister, he offered Northcliffe a post in his Cabinet which he declined and became Minister for Propaganda. He agreed to head the British War Mission in the USA for which service he became Viscount Northcliffe in 1918. With the end of the war in sight, his desire to be at the forefront of the political scene, now led him into two confrontations, first with Sir Edward Carson and then with Lloyd George. Northcliffe ended up suffering two very public humiliations.

Northcliffe was very keen to be part of the British Delegation at the forthcoming Peace Conference. He published his Peace Terms in his newspapers, which became known as "Northcliffe's Thirteen Points". At the same time, he attacked Lord Milner, the

War Minister. Milner had suggested that, because of the fear of Bolshevism, conditional peace terms for Germany should be imposed. This was described by Northcliffe as "Milner's Blunder" and "Milner's Mischief." *The Evening News* warned that "his (Milner's) German origin is not forgotten and the man in the street declares that he is acting like a Prussian. Lord Milner should take care. If this impression were to spread, the results might surprise him."[173] Sir Edward Carson was determined to put Northcliffe in his place.

In a stinging rebuke he said: "I am quite alive to the fact that it is almost high treason to say a word against Lord Northcliffe. I know his power and that he does not hesitate to try to drive anybody out of any office or a public position if they incur his royal displeasure. Within the last few days there has been an attack made by this Noble Lord's papers upon Lord Milner. Lord Milner is Secretary of State for War and if Lord Northcliffe is not a Minister – as I believe he says he is not a Minister – he is at least an official of one of the Government Ministers. Lord Milner seems to have given an interview to a rival paper. Having read it and having read the criticism of some of Lord Northcliffe's papers upon it, I believe that it has been purposely and intentionally misrepresented and misunderstood. I think it is really time to put an end to that kind of thing. I believe that all the best elements in the country resent this kind of thing. Everyone knows, who has been in public life or in public office, that the moment that Lord Northcliffe's displeasure is incurred, from that moment onwards a kind of man-hunt occurs, until he drives anybody, whom he looks upon as an adversary, out of office—he is anxious to drive Lord Milner out of office—for what? In order that Lord Northcliffe may get it or may get into the War Cabinet so that he may be present at the Peace Conference. The whole thing is a disgrace to public life in England and a disgrace to journalism."[174]

---

173 Lee Thompson. p 309
174 House of Commons Debates Series 5 Vol 110 cols 2350-2352 7 November 1918

But this was nothing compared with the attack on Northcliffe by Lloyd George in the House of Commons on 16 April 1919. Lloyd George had been incensed by the repeated attacks by the Northcliffe newspapers on the proposed Peace Terms, more particularly when Northcliffe demanded, as the price of his support for the Government, that he should be member of the Peace Delegation. Lloyd George said about Northcliffe: "Reliable! That is the last adjective I would use. It is here today, jumping there to-morrow and there the next day. I would as soon rely on a grasshopper. Still, I am prepared to make some allowance—even great newspapers will forgive me for saying so—when a man is labouring under a keen sense of disappointment, however unjustified, however ridiculous the expectations may have been, he is always apt to think the world is badly run. When a man has deluded himself, and all the people whom he ever permits to go near to him, help him into the belief that he is the only man who can win the War, and he is waiting for the clamour of the multitude that is going to demand his presence there to direct the destinies of the world, and there is not a whisper, not a sound, it is rather disappointing; it is unnerving; it is upsetting."

"When the War is won without him, there must be something wrong. Of course it must be the Government, when at any rate he is the only one to make peace. The only people who get near him tell him so, constantly tell him so. So he publishes the Peace Terms and waits for the "call". It does not come. He retreats to sunny climes, waiting, but not a sound reaches that far-distant shore to call him back to the great task of saving the world. What can you expect? He comes back and he says "Well I cannot see the disaster but I am sure it is there, it is bound to come." Under these conditions I am prepared to make allowances; but let me say this, that when that kind of diseased vanity—". (Lloyd George then tapped his finger on the top of his head to indicate that he thought Northcliffe was now deranged). Lloyd George then turned to the newspapers themselves. "They still believe in France that *The Times* is a serious organ. They do not know that it is merely a threepenny edition of *The Daily Mail; that* is my only apology for giving notice of that kind of trash, with which some of these papers have been filled during the last few weeks."[175] Megalomania contributed to a nervous breakdown shortly before Northcliffe's death in 1922. As a predator seeking the prey of controlling Governments and directing policy, he was ultimately unsuccessful. Hugh Cudlipp, the famous editor of *"The Daily Mirror"*, described Northcliffe "as a man corrupted by power and wealth, who desecrated journalistic standards and became dominated by the pursuit of political power, unguided by political prescience."[176]

Harold Harmsworth, later Lord Rothermere, Northcliffe's brother, started an affair in 1925 with Princess Stephanie von Hohenlohe, a glamorous Austrian Princess, who was a German spy. She later became London's leading Nazi hostess. The affair lasted until 1939. But like his brother, Rothermere's power was not directed to sex but to seeking to run government policy by the weight of newspaper ownership. He and Northcliffe disliked Haig and did their best to get him removed from command of the BEF in 1918. Trenchard had been a successful commander of the Royal Flying Corps in France. He was described as "providing the strong far sighted leadership required by the Air Arm in its infant days."[177] In 1917, the RFC and the Royal Naval Air Service were merged into the RAF. Trenchard was succeeded by Salmond. There was political manoeuvring and speculation about the new posts of Air Minister, Chief of Air Staff and senior positions in the new Air Ministry. Rothermere became Air Minister in December 1917, on Lloyd George's recommendation. Rothermere invited Trenchard to London and offered him the post of the Chief of the Air Staff. Rothermere explained that Trenchard's support would be useful to him as he, Rothermere was about to launch a Press campaign against Haig and Robertson (Chief of the General

---

175 House of Commons Debates Series 5 Vol 114 cols. 2952-2953 19 April 1919
176 Lee Thompson p xii
177 Terraine, John. *The Smoke and the Fire.*(Sidgwick and Jackson. London 1980) p188.

Staff). Trenchard refused the job. He was loyal to Haig and did not believe in political intrigue. Rothermere and Northcliffe spent the rest of the day acrimoniously debating with Trenchard. They threatened that, if he did not accept, they would attack Haig, alleging that Haig had refused to release Trenchard. Eventually Trenchard, while vigorously defending Haig, agreed to take the post, provided that he got Haig's consent, which he did.[178] Trenchard and Rothermere unsurprisingly could not get on, resulting in their both resigning in April1918. Trenchard subsequently had a very distinguished career in the RAF but Rothermere was to suffer public humiliation.

While the Amalgamated Press grew in size, it gradually diminished in authority which its supine support for the Nazi regime did nothing to enhance. Born in 1868, Harmsworth was created Viscount Rothermere in 1919, having served as President of the Air Council in Lloyd George's Government during the war. A description of him, shortly after the war, appears in Duff Cooper's diaries. The entry for 1 December 1920 reads: "We dined with—and Rothermere. The last named is, I think, one of the most repulsive men I ever met. He looks like a pig and when not speaking, snores quietly to himself. He is rude, pompous, extremely stupid, common beyond any other member of his family and beyond belief, utterly devoid of the slightest streak of humour or dash of originality."[179]

By 1931, the Conservatives under Baldwin were slowly recovering from defeat at the polls two years previously. Among the many issues facing the Conservatives was the question of the future of India but more immediately was the perennial argument between the proponents of free trade and protectionism. At the forefront of this latter debate were the two press Barons, Beaverbrook and Rothermere. "Empire Free Trade" was their rallying cry. An Empire Crusade and United Empire Party were started. Rothermere went even further. On 5 January 1930, the

---

178 Boyle,Andrew. *Trenchard, Man of Vision.*(Collins, London.1962) pp 245-255
179 *The Duff Cooper Diaries*(Phoenix, London 2006) p 136

leader in *The Daily Mail* read: "There is no man living in this country today with more likelihood of succeeding to the Premiership of Great Britain than Lord Beaverbrook".

At Twickenham in 1929, the Conservative candidate, converted to support Empire Free Trade, nearly lost a safe seat. Free Trade candidates sponsored by Beaverbrook and Rothermere stood at Bromley, Islington East and Paddington South. At Bromley the Conservatives had a reduced majority. At Islington East, the Empire Crusade candidate split the vote and Labour took the seat from the Conservatives. At Paddington South, the Conservatives lost the seat to the Empire Crusade. When the seat at St George's Westminster (a safe Conservative seat) fell vacant, the scene was set for a battle between Baldwin and the Press Barons. Because of Baldwin's unpopularity and the viciousness of the Press attacks on him, there was great reluctance on the part of Conservatives to stand as candidates, even though, in 1929, the Conservative candidate had secured 78% of the votes.

Duff Cooper, nursing a safe seat at Winchester, bravely volunteered to stand at St George's. His opponent stood as an independent Conservative, but in truth the latter was persuaded by Beaverbrook and Rothermere to stand, supporting Empire Crusade. They had been responsible for his address and secretly agreed to pay all his election expenses and supported him at meetings. Two days before the poll, *The Daily Mail,* in an article signed by the editor, sneered that the Conservative leader could hardly be a fit person to restore the fortunes of the country when he had lost his own personal fortune. Baldwin hit back: "The papers conducted by Lord Rothermere and Lord Beaverbrook are not newspapers in the ordinary acceptance of the term.— What are their methods? Their methods are direct falsehood, misrepresentation, half-truths, the alteration of the speaker's meaning by publishing a sentence apart from the context such as you see in these leaflets handed outside the doors of this hall; suppression and editorial criticism of speeches, which are not reported in the press......"

Baldwin then turned to *The Daily Mail* article: "I have no idea of the name of that gentleman. I would only observe that he is well qualified for the post which he holds. The first part of the statement is a lie—the paragraph could only have been written by a cad—I am advised that an action for libel would lie. I shall not move in the matter and for this reason; I should get an apology and heavy damages. The first is of no value, and the second I would not touch with a barge pole. What the proprietorship of these papers is aiming at, is power and power without responsibility,—the prerogative of the harlot throughout the ages." On polling day, Duff Cooper was elected.

Rothermere never really recovered from this public humiliation and his influence on the political scene thereafter, seriously declined, almost certainly accelerated by his uncritical devotion to the Nazi regime. This had its origin in his meeting with Princess Stephanie van Hohenlohe in 1925. She was born in Vienna in 1891 of partial Jewish descent. As a teenager, she enrolled in the ballet school of the Vienna Court Opera. She gradually became part of Vienna's high society and in her early twenties she began an affair with the Archduke Franz Salvador, Prince of Tuscany and the son-in-law of the Emperor. The Archduke was married and, when she was pregnant with his child, a scandal had to be averted. In May 1914, she was married to a German Prince, Friedrich Franz von Hohenlohe, in London. Her son was born in December 1914.

After the war she took Hungarian citizenship and, in 1920, divorced her husband. She then went to live in France. In 1925, she met Rothermere in Monte Carlo. He had already shown enthusiasm for ballet dancers like Nikitina and had had other mistresses, but he was immediately attracted to the Princess and lavished money and jewellery on her. He set her up at the Dorchester Hotel and asked her to act as a sort of roving Ambassador. She was to use her rich contacts in Europe, to provide him with information for his papers. She persuaded him to take up the cudgels on behalf of Hungary, which had lost territory as a result of the Peace Treaty. More particularly she had valuable contacts in the upcoming Nazi hierarchy. Despite her Jewish background, she was on the friendliest terms not only with Hitler, but also with Ribbentrop, Goering and Himmler.

The relationship benefitted both Rothermere and the Princess. He found her useful in establishing personal contact with Hitler and other influential Nazis and naturally enjoyed a pleasant relationship with her. She was able, living in London to act as a propagandist for the Hitler regime and to act as a spy, meeting many businessmen and politicians in positions of influence. In July 1932, Rothermere agreed to pay her an annual retainer of £5000 and £2000 for each assignment.[180] When, in 1939, the relationship broke up and he ceased paying, she claimed that he had promised to pay the retainer for the rest of her life. Her claim failed. That she was a German spy is not in doubt. In the 1920s she was monitored by the British authorities who regarded her as an extremely dangerous person. In 1932 she had been forced to leave France because the French believed she was involved in espionage. When she went to the United States during the war, she was also regarded by the authorities there, as extremely dangerous, intelligent and clever, and as a spy worse than ten thousand men.

Rothermere's enthusiasm for the Nazi regime was only partly due to his infatuation with the Princess. Rothermere supported the British Union of Fascists and wrote a *"Daily Mail"* editorial "Hurrah for the Blackshirts". He had welcomed Hitler's rise to power, writing an article under the headline "A Nation Reborn", "Youth Asserting Its Power" and "New Chapter in Europe's History". In July 1933, he wrote a leader from "Somewhere in Naziland", with a headline "Youth triumphant." He said "Any minor misdeeds of individual Nazis would be submerged by the immense benefits the new regime is already bestowing upon Germany."[181] Rothermere thereafter regularly corresponded with Hitler, exchanging gifts with him, including a priceless Gobelin tapestry and a jade bowl.

Thanks to the Princess, he visited Hitler on a number of occasions. He and Hitler had met for the first time in Berlin in December 1934, when Rothermere gave a dinner party for him

---

180 Taylor. S.J. *The Great Outsiders* (Weidenfeld & Nicolson. London 1996) p 292
181 Ibid. p 290-292

and other Nazi officials. Between 1933 and 1938 Rothermere and Hitler conducted a private correspondence. In June 1933, Hitler had sent a signed photo of himself as an appreciation of two supportive articles written by Rothermere in *The Daily Mail*. In March 1934, Hitler wrote: "I have already impressed on the kind bearer of your letter and gifts how greatly I would be pleased to confide to you personally, Lord Rothermere, if a visit to Germany were possible—." In April 1935, Rothermere wrote to Hitler: "I esteem it a great honour and privilege to be in correspondence with your Excellency—I hope your Excellency is taking great care of yourself." In April 1936, Rothermere sent good wishes to Hitler on his electoral success and for his birthday. It was the month when German troops marched into the Rhineland in breach of the Treaty of Versailles.

His birthday wishes to Hitler in April 1937 could not have been more effusive: "May I join the myriad of those who on your birthday will be wishing you long life to crown your efforts to achieve good government, liberty and peace." After Munich in September 1938, Hitler wrote "I appreciate your hopes that I should become as popular in England as Frederick the Great, was. Your reference to Adolf the Great is also very flattering."[182] *The Daily Mail* consistently took the view that German intentions were peaceful. In May 1938, Rothermere had written an article headlined: "CZECHOSLOVAKIA NOT OUR BUSINESS", a copy of which was signed by the editor and sent to the German Ambassador in London. In 1937, the Princess had arranged visits by Halifax (Foreign Secretary) to meet Goering and for the Duke and Duchess of Windsor to meet Hitler. It was in this year also, that she began another affair, this time with Fritz Wiedemann, a personal aide to Hitler. When he became Consul General in San Francisco, she joined him for a while, then returned to England, leaving at the outbreak of war and rejoining Fritz in America. Eventually, she was arrested and interned as an enemy alien. After the war, she returned to Germany where she worked for a number of publishing companies. She died in 1972.

---

182 Ibid pp 294 -298

Although the Harmsworths both had extramarital affairs, the aphrodisiac in their cases was not primarily sexual. What drove them was the desire for power and influence in the political world. The power they sought and indeed tried to exercise was the power to control governments and to dictate government policies. That they both failed in somewhat humiliating fashion merely serves to confirm the view that a self-righteous belief in your own importance does not necessarily carry with it a guarantee of success. The Harmsworths are now mere footnotes in history.

CHAPTER THIRTEEN

PAUL REYNAUD AND THE COMTESSE HELENE PORTES

Paul Reynaud was Prime Minister of France in the spring of 1940, during the critical months of the war, when the German Army overwhelmed the French and forced them to ask for an armistice. Behind Reynaud was the rather sinister figure of his mistress, Helene Portes, who was a well-known German sympathiser. Her influence on his decisions, at a momentous time for France, was totally malevolent. Reynaud had been born in October 1878. His father ran a successful textile business and Reynaud was sent to the Sorbonne to study law. He was small in stature and was called variously a "pocket Napoleon" or "Micky Mouse". He had a brilliant intellect and was a formidable debater but he lacked charm. He liked nothing better than a fight. Because he spent a good deal of time manoeuvring for political advancement, he eventually found himself without a party.

When he had entered politics in 1919, he leant towards the right, becoming a member, and subsequently vice president, of the centre right Democratic Republican Alliance party. While, initially, he had been sympathetic to the problems of German reparations in the 1920s, he became alarmed in the 1930s by the spectre of a resurgent Germany. He was a supporter of closer links with Britain and Russia as a counter to this threat and strongly opposed appeasement. He held a number of cabinet posts in the early 1930s, but his views about the necessity for rearmament, because of German aggression towards Austria and Czechoslovakia, did not endear him to members of his party. It was not until 1938 that he returned to the cabinet as Minister of Finance in Daladier's government. After the Sudeten crisis, he became Minister of Justice but subsequently left the party to become an independent. However after the collapse of the socialist government of Blum in 1938, Daladier appointed him Minister of Finance.

French finances in the 1930 had been close to bankruptcy on a number of occasions. Devaluation of the franc was a familiar economic device. Industrial output had been sluggish and a regulatory policy of business affairs, much favoured by Blum's government, had proved unsuccessful. Reynaud's programme of deregulation was not only popular but was broadly successful. An austerity programme was enforced and at the outbreak of war in 1939, France's economic outlook had improved enormously. In March 1940, Reynaud became premier in succession to Daladier, but only by a single vote, and the Chamber of Deputies insisted on Daladier being Minister of National Defence and Minister of War. In May 1940, the Germans invaded France and defeated the Allied forces. Reynaud sacked General Gamelin, then Commander in Chief of the French Army, and appointed Marshall Petain, the hero of the First World War to be Minister of State. Helene had known the Marshall from childhood and when he arrived in Paris in May, she is said to have greeted him with the words "Monsieur Marshall, stop Reynaud making a fool of himself."[183] When, in June 1940. Paris fell to the Germans, the question arose of whether France could continue to fight and whether she had the will to do so. It was in this situation that the malevolent influence of Helene, Reynaud's mistress, played a leading part.

Helene Portes was the daughter of a businessman from Marseilles. She had been introduced to Reynaud by Andre Tardieu in the early 1930s and from 1938 she and Reynaud lived together. She was one of a number of powerful women who, in that period, exercised enormous power over French political leaders. The others were Madame Bonnet, who was the mistress of Georges Bonnet, sometime Minister for Foreign affairs and the Marquise de Crussol, mistress of Daladier, who had held all the main offices

183 Tellier, Thibault. *Paul Reynaud* (Layard, Paris 2005) p 582

of state at different times. Because Helene's family had a sardine canning business, she was known vulgarly as "la sardine qui s'est crue sole."[184] The Marquise and Helene were bitter rivals and, in early January 1940, Helene began a campaign to seek to replace Daladier as premier and to install Reynaud in his place. She ran an exclusive salon where she complained of Daladier's lethargy, which was duly reported by the Marquise to Daladier.[185] When Reynaud invited socialists into his cabinet, Helene wrote to him from Arcachon: "You have taken advantage of my absence to allow Marxists to enter the cabinet. You will not resist the blows of these people."[186] She was ever present at the decisions taken by Reynaud as Premier.

On 6 June 1940, the American Ambassador in France telegraphed President Roosevelt to say that: "that the French who are beaten, deserve better than to be governed by the Premier's mistress. This evening Reynaud forbade her to come into the room, where he was going to telephone you. Nevertheless, she came in and, when he ordered her to leave the room, she refused. I think in future you should avoid such conversations because the woman in question will tell the whole world and exaggerate."[187] She was said to have had a liaison with the German Ambassador and wanted to distance herself from Jews and old politicians. She was against Reynaud having aides who favoured a strong military stance. She used to read secret documents in bed and purporting to be acting on behalf of Reynaud sought information from the head of the German section of French intelligence.[188]

Reynaud and Helene lived in his flat near the Assembly, where he worked, and she constantly rang him or appeared in his office. She was strongly anti-British, a tendency which increased as the

184 "The sardine who thinks she is a sole"
185 Home, Alistair. *To Lose a Battle*. (Macmillan and Co Ltd. London 1969) p153.
186 Guichard, Jean-Pierre. *Paul Reynaud*. (L. Harmattan. Paris. 2008.) p117
187 Bullit, William. *For The President*. (Houghton-Mifflin co. Boston. USA 1972) p 175
188 Fenby, Jonathan. *The History of Modern France*. (Simon and Schuster. London 2015.) p 272

war moved on. On one occasion, when Reynaud was in bed unwell, the centre of power moved from his office to his flat, where Helene took charge. A journalist, Pierre Lazareff, wanted an interview with Reynaud. Helene answered the phone and told him that they were overwhelmed but to come anyway. He did."[189] When he arrived, he found Helen sitting behind Reynaud's work desk. She was holding a meeting surrounded by senior officers, deputies and civil servants. She spoke a lot, very quickly in a peremptory tone, giving advice and orders. From time to time she opened the door of his room and was heard to say—"How are you Paul. Sleep well. Sleep well. Let us get on with our work."[190]

Reynaud's reaction to the disasters which had beset his country was to fight to the end, and, if, necessary from the colonies in Africa. France and Britain had previously entered into a treaty forbidding a separate peace or armistice. However his efforts were severely handicapped by the intrigues of Helene, who believed that an armistice must be sought at all costs. She was supported by a combination of Petain, General Weygand and Paul Baudouin who, although only an undersecretary, was strongly under Helene's influence. Baudouin described her as "acting like a president of the Cabinet."[191] General Spears had been liaison officer with the French Army in 1914 and again in 1939. He reported that, as soon as any of the British left after discussions with Reynaud, Helene would rush in and ask what had been said and assailed him: "What did he say" What is the sense of going on? Thousands of men are being killed while you hesitate to stop the war."[192]

She was described by Spears as "ugly, mal soignée, dirty, nasty and half demented and a sore trial." Spears added "Helene had done Reynaud more harm than good for it was she who had imposed on him, as collaborators, the men who were now his

---

189 Guichard, p 172
190 Ibid p 173
191 Ibid p 126
192 Spears, Major General Sir Edward. *Assignment to Catastrophe.* (Heinemann Ltd London 1954) vol 2 p196.

bitterest enemies."[193] Another view expressed by the first secretary to the American Ambassador was "It is necessary not to underestimate the role which she played in encouraging the defeatist elements during Reynaud's last days as Premier. She knew all our efforts were in the opposite direction, but she was in a state of panic, such that she wished to miss no opportunity to persuade Reynaud to throw in the sponge.—I myself saw Reynaud at least four times a day, for several days as Premier, and there was never an occasion when Helene did not just happen to come into his office. And, I believe that, if little by little he lost his judgement, it was mainly because of the influence which she exercised over him."[194]

A good example of her influence was her role in securing the dismissal of Alexis Leger from the highly influential post of Secretary General of the Foreign Office by publicly issuing several vituperative criticisms of him.[195] More importantly, in June 1940, at the gravest time for France, Reynaud attempted to negotiate with De Gaulle to reorganize the French forces and, once again, Helene interfered. De Gaulle described arriving in Chissay, and that, when Helene arrived, "all their work was undone". She agreed with Georges Mandel that: "We have had enough of your politics and you politicians. We must have an armistice and an armistice at any price". She added, pointing at De Gaulle: "There is a man who wants to play at being a politician. Let him put himself at the head of his tanks and prove himself on the battlefield."[196]

On 15 June 1940, Helene had even imagined a government presided over by Petain in which Reynaud became vice president, bringing his experience behind the scenes. To that end, she had spoken directly to Petain to get him constantly to provoke a ministerial crisis, to speed up the fall of the cabinet. On 16 June 1940, Churchill suggested to Reynaud an indissoluble union between France and Britain. Reynaud was enthusiastic. When

193 Ibid p280
194 Tellier. p 545-546
195 Ibid p 583
196 Ibid p 653

Helene learnt that Reynaud was going to propose an emergency Franco-British Union, she sent a message to him while he was in the Council of Ministers, saying: "I hope you are not going to play the part of Isabeau of Bavaria." This was a reference to the involvement of Isabeau of Bavaria, the wife of mad King Charles VI of France, in negotiating in his absence a peace treaty in 1420 with England – the Treaty of Troyes, for which thereafter she was ever held responsible for having sworn away the crown of France. Helene insisted on seeing the text before it was announced to the French Cabinet. She notified the defeatists in the Cabinet before the meeting. In the result, the Cabinet rejected the idea.[197] Reynaud resigned, to Helene's delight.

She had family in America and had applied for a visa to go there. It was proposed that Reynaud should become the French Ambassador to Washington. It was not to be. While driving together to escape the Germans, the car overturned and Helene was killed. Reynaud now remained in France. He was arrested by the Germans and imprisoned throughout the war. After the war, he went back into politics. In 1946, he was elected a member of the Chamber of Deputies. He held several cabinet posts but his attempts to form a government in 1952 and 1953 ended in failure. He left office in 1962 and died in 1966.

In this case, it is clear that, unlike many of the other examples of politicians and their mistresses, Helene was the predator and Reynaud the prey.

---

197 Fenby, p 275

CHAPTER FOURTEEN

LORD BEAVERBROOK

Max Aitken, subsequently Lord Beaverbrook, had a meteoric career in politics as well as being the proprietor of *The Express* newspapers. Born in Canada in 1879, he became in turns a millionaire, statesman and historian. His father had moved from Scotland to Canada in 1864 and at the time of Aitken's birth was in charge of St James' Church in Newcastle, New Brunswick. Aitken had a number of ventures as a young man, entering law school, helping a friend's political career and selling life insurance. But, when he was twenty one, he became a travelling salesman of bonds working on a commission. It was a time when the Canadian economy was expanding exponentially. He bought a number of companies, which did not seem to be very flourishing. He, subsequently sold his shares, now profitable, to buy other companies. Others had seen the prospect of an economic boom and Aitken was not alone in becoming rich. Aided by a wealthy financier from Halifax, Aitken became in charge of the "Royal Securities Corporation" and invested in other companies. Although he had a salary of only $4,000, he owned shares which by 1907 meant that he was a dollar millionaire. But the shareholders were constantly being obstructive and, when he moved to Montreal, he ceased to be a company promoter and became an investment banker. In 1906 he had married Dorothy Drury. It was not to be a great success.

He did not find banking successful and moved back to Royal Securities Corporation without the problem of other shareholders. In 1908, after an introduction from Ian Hamilton Benn, a strong Unionist in the City of London, Aitken came to London and, with

Benn's assistance, involved himself in making money. He continued with mergers all over Canada, ending up with the acquisition of the Steel Company of Canada. The hostility which these ventures incurred were to lead to accusations against Aitken of some shady dealings, more particularly in 1911, when the affairs of the Canada Cement Company, which he had formed, fell into disarray.

In 1910, Aitken left Canada, never to take up permanent residence there again. He had an introduction to Bonar Law, a leading Conservative politician in England, who was to befriend him and become one of his financial backers. But it was a City acquaintance, Edward Goulding, MP for Worcester, who persuaded Aitken to enter politics and the law, found him a seat to contest at Ashton–under-Lyne. Here Aitken became an MP with a majority of 196. Shortly afterwards, Aitken was given the opportunity to buy *The Daily Express* which was in financial difficulties. Subsequently, he also bought *The Globe*.

In April, 1911, he was offered a knighthood by the Conservatives "rewarding him for services to come and to the Unionist party."[198] Bonar Law recorded: "as regards Sir Max Aitken, he is the most intimate personal friend I have in the House of Commons (in spite of the comparatively short time I have known him) and not only for that reason, but because of his remarkable force and ability."[199] Aitken also played a prominent part in the resignation of Asquith in 1916 as Prime Minister and his replacement by Lloyd George. He was then offered a peerage by Lloyd George and became Lord Beaverbrook. In 1918, Lloyd George made him Minister of Information and Chancellor of the Duchy of Lancaster.

After the war, Beaverbrook continued to take a full part in political affairs. He attended the Peace Conference. He was instrumental in the appointment of Bonar Law as Prime Minister and, subsequently, with the help of his newspapers, *The Daily and Sunday Express*, he began a campaign in support of legislation to

---

198 Taylor A.J.P *Beaverbrook* (Hamish Hamilton. London 1972.) p 60
199 Ibid p 71

afford protection to trade from the colonies, "The Empire Crusade". To this end he supported a number of candidates at by-elections against the government of Baldwin. After some success, he was defeated by Baldwin in 1932 at the St George's Westminster by-election during which Baldwin made his famous and successful attack on newspaper proprietors (Beaverbrook and Rothermere) already referred to in a previous chapter, with his immortal comment: "what the proprietorship of these papers is aiming at is power, but power without responsibility—the prerogative of the harlot throughout the ages." Thereafter the campaign faltered and a truce with Baldwin was made.

During the Second World War, Beaverbrook became Minister of Aircraft production and is credited with ensuring an increased number of fighter aircraft. When he resigned in April 1941, he was made Minister of State and continued to have a seat in the War Cabinet. When Russia was invaded in June 1941, he became Minister of Supply. In that capacity he was responsible for ensuring that both Britain and Russia received materials from the United States. He was present during the meeting between Churchill and Roosevelt giving rise to the Atlantic Charter. A subsequent mission to Moscow was a great success. He now left the Government and went on a mission to Washington. Thereafter, in 1942, he became Lord Privy Seal with responsibility for post war civil aviation. After the war, he had no political appointment but used his newspapers to project his views. *The Express* papers were at that time probably the most powerful and certainly the most popular. He wrote a series of books about politicians and about the war which were much acclaimed.

Apart from his wife, there were four particular women with whom he enjoyed a sexual relationship. He also had a number of lady friends to whom he gave substantial presents and financial advice. Venetia Montagu, Jean Norton, Lilly Ernst and Dorothy Hall were among them. Venetia had married Edwin Montagu in 1915, after ceasing to be Asquith's mistress. By 1917 the marriage was in serious trouble and her affair with Beaverbrook probably started in 1918. When Beaverbrook went to Paris for the Peace Conference, he was living openly with Venetia while her husband resided at a different hotel. Diana Cooper wrote to Duff Cooper on 14 January 1919: "Crooks (Beaverbrook) and Venetia turned up just as we were turning out. It was a disgusting case—her face lights up when that animated little deformity so much as turns to her. They are living in open sin at the Ritz in a tall silk suite, with a common bath and unlocked doors between, while poor Ted is sardined, into the Majestic, unknown and uncared for."[200]

When Diana visited Venetia at the Ritz "she could hear Crooks' ablutions next door." On one occasion, after they had all dined together, Diana wrote: " I have just left Crooks and V in their luxurious nest and expedited Ted to his Etoile."[201] Venetia supplied Beaverbrook with some of Asquith's letters and some Cabinet documents which Asquith had sent her, When Beaverbrook's wife died in 1927, he turned in despair to Venetia and she gave him great comfort,[202] Beaverbrook for his part provided financial assistance to Venetia and also to Edwin. He helped her with her investments, showered her with presents and took her on holidays. They kept up a passionate correspondence until her death in 1948.

It was in 1925 that he first became enamoured of another married woman who was to be his prime passion for the next twenty years. Jean Norton had been married to Richard, the heir to Lord Grantley, for some six years. They had two young children. The Nortons, though not particularly wealthy, were very much part of the grand London social scene. Jean, aged twenty seven, was strikingly attractive and the Nortons became friends of Beaverbrook. He arranged for Jean to run one of his cinemas, while Richard found other pursuits. Beaverbrook's wife, Gladys, took herself off to Canada for a period in 1926 and 1927 while he entertained Jean at his house in Surrey. When Gladys returned in 1927, she was taken seriously ill with a brain tumour and

---

200 Cooper, Artemis (Ed) *A Durable Fire. The Letters of Duff and Diana Cooper 1913-1950*. (Franklin Watts. Inc. New York 1984) p 131
201 Ibid pp 131/132.
202 Chisholm, Ann & Davie, Michael. *Beaverbrook. A Life*. (Hutchinson Publishing Company Ltd. London 1992) p 261

died in December. Guilt and grief in equal measure overcame Beaverbrook.

After a short visit to the United States and Canada, he resumed his affair with Jean while remaining on good terms with Richard. She, for her part, looked after the children and they had a busy social life but managed to meet Richard regularly; they dined together; they stayed together and they travelled together. It was not, by all accounts, a particularly smooth relationship. She was upset by Beaverbrook's interest in other women which was a constant source of friction and she was anxious about money. Beaverbrook was always generous in money matters and Jean, as well as Richard, was a beneficiary.

Largesse on a grand scale was one form of the exercise of power by Beaverbrook. There was a particular row in 1931. Jean was having a good social life and Beaverbrook resented this, because it was paid for by his money. He wanted to go to Canada and she didn't. She nearly left him. In the end, he went without her. There was another row when Beaverbrook introduced her to Dorothy Hall, whom he had met on his way back from New York in 1931. Dorothy Hall was a 28 year old, rich American, unhappily married with two children and independent of Beaverbrook's generosity. They fell for each other and after going to Paris together, she joined him in London. Unsurprisingly Jean did not take the presence of a rival with equanimity and, after a row, took herself off to Paris. When she returned, she found that Dorothy had left for America and her relationship with Beaverbrook was restored. The affair with Dorothy was effectively over, though they continued to remain friends. She subsequently became the owner of *The New York Post*. The affair with Jean continued for some 17 years with frequent rows over Beaverbrook's attention to other women. Daphne Weymouth, Sibell Lygon, Harriet Cohen, Virginia West and Diana Cooper were just a few of those to whom Beaverbrook paid court.

But a more enduring affair was with Lily Ernst. She was a Hungarian Jewess, who lived in Vienna. In 1937 she was in an Austrian ballet company performing in the south of France. There she met Beaverbrook. After Beaverbrook returned to London, he suddenly had a fancy to see the dancers again. He discovered that Lily was engaged and they parted, with Beaverbrook telling her that he would always be a good friend.[203] In May 1938, after the Anschluss, she got in touch with Beaverbrook, who arranged for her to come to England, She was in love with him and eventually he fell in love with her, much to Jean's fury. They continued as lovers during the war and, she hoped to take Jean' place but the affair had run its course. Before she married Anthony Hornby in 1949, it is thought that Beaverbrook had himself proposed to her. He continued to send letters and presents to her. But it was Jean who occupied his life throughout the war. She wrote on one occasion: "I can say no more than that I am and always shall be your ever loving, Jeannie." When she died, Beaverbrook wrote to Diana Cooper: "I have lost my moorings,"[204] Sir James Dunn had been an old friend and, when he died in January 1956, his widow, Christofor, and Beaverbrook became close and they started living together. In June 1963 they were married. On 9 June 1964 he died at the age of 85.

203 Chisholm p 345
204 Ibid p 452

CHAPTER FIFTEEN

MUSSOLINI

Mussolini, the founder of Italian Fascism was the Prime Minister, Head of Government and under the title of Il Duce, the all-powerful dictator of Italy from 1923 until his death in July 1943. While he had a number of affairs, his four most prominent mistresses were Ida Dalser, Angelica Balabanoff, Cesare Sarfati and Clara Petacci. The latter was immensely loyal and was with him when he was captured by partisans in 1943. They died together.

Mussolini was born in July 1883, the son of a blacksmith who was a socialist. His mother was a Catholic schoolteacher. He used to help his father in the smithy. He was expelled from two schools, on each occasion for stabbing a fellow student with a knife.[205] Thereafter, as a day boy, he did better and qualified as an elementary schoolmaster. In 1902, partly to avoid National Service, he emigrated to Switzerland where he led a vagrant's life. He became violently anti-capitalist. He spoke publicly about the need for the use of violence and advocated a general strike. He was arrested for fighting a duel and deported but, on his return to Switzerland was again arrested, this time for false documents and went back to Italy.[206] He served for two years in the Army where he had a reputation as a revolutionary. He then returned to teaching. He was not a successful teacher and found himself unable to maintain order.[207]

205 Monelli, Paolo. *Mussolini. An Intimate Life.* (Thames and Hudson. London 1953) p 29
206 Kirkpatrick, Sir Ivone. *Mussolini* (Odhams Books Ltd, London 1964) p 42.
207 Mack Smith, Denis. *Mussolini* (Vintage Books, New York. 1983) p 10

From 1909, he became the publisher and editor of a number of radical newspapers, periodicals, books and articles. He was now a prominent socialist. He took part in protests against the government's war in Tripoli, for which he was imprisoned for five months. He started a paper called *Avanti*, whose assistant editor was Angelica Balabanoff. She became his mistress, as did Margheritti Sarfatti, who was the art critic. She remained his mistress until the 1930s.

In 1914, Italy entered the war on the side of the Allies. Mussolini strongly supported that view, which was not held by all in the Socialist party. Eventually he was expelled from the party. He now became increasingly more nationalistic and advocated the idea of a vanguard elite to lead society, the beginnings of Fascism. After the rout of the Italian army at Caporetto in October 1917, the British, through Sir Samuel Hoare (then a staff officer in Italy), obtained permission from MI5 to provide Mussolini with funds (said to be £100 a week) to finance propaganda for the war.[208]. The crisis passed. There was also some suggestion that the French had bribed Mussolini, at the beginning of the war, to persuade his paper to support the war.[209] Mussolini himself served for nine months in the Army before being invalided out.

In March 1919, Mussolini launched a movement that was to become, two years, later the fascist party. Supported by armed gangs of war veterans called Blackshirts, Mussolini began to organise the fascist party to seize power. He himself was elected to the Chamber of Deputies in 1921. In 1922 the fascists marched on Rome and ousted the Prime Minister, Luigi Facia. King Victor Emmanuel III, who had the executive and military authority, handed over his power and invited Mussolini to become Prime Minister and to form a new government. Although his government was a coalition in which the fascist party were in a minority, it was Mussolini's intention to set up a totalitarian state over which he would preside as leader ("Il Duce"). Opposition was met by force. After the elections in 1924 when the fascists won

---

208 Ibid p 81
209 Ibid pp 64 -73

the majority of seats, the Socialist leader, Matteoti, who had denounced the elections because of intimidation, was murdered (on Mussolini's orders).

Mussolini gradually took over the important ministries and the police authorities, so that, by 1927, all constitutional restraints had been removed from government and Mussolini became a dictator, not only in name, but in fact. He was no longer answerable to parliament but only to the King. Parliamentary elections were abolished and a Grand Council of Fascism simply selected a single list of candidates to be approved by a plebiscite. He pursued an aggressive foreign policy, designed to improve Italy's standing in the world. In 1923, the murder of an Italian General on Greek territory was used as an excuse by Italy to invade and bombard Corfu. After occupying the Island for a month, the army withdrew. His actions were condemned at the League of Nations and many regarded it as a failure, but Mussolini acquired much prestige from the populace.[210] He secured great influence in Albania and in Libya sought to exercise much more control over the colony.

Ida Dalser was a lover of Mussolini and probably his first wife. She was born in August 1880, near Trento, the daughter of the village Mayor. As a teenager, she was sent to Paris to study cosmetic medicine. When she came back she opened a French-style beauty salon in Milan. In about 1909, they started a relationship and when he was refused employment, because of his socialist political activities, she supported him from the proceeds of her salon. She was described as "not particularly good looking but with a certain intelligence and impulsive charm. She was jealous of Rachele Gudi (whom he had married in December 1915), and intemperate in her demands on Mussolini"[211] It appears that Ida and Mussolini were married in 1914. On 11 November 1915, she gave birth to a son, Benito. In September 1915, Rachele had also given birth to a son by Mussolini, In January 1916, Mussolini recognised Benito before notaries as

---

210 Mack Smith p 72
211 Kirkpatrick. P 73

his son and was ordered to pay an allowance to Ida of 200 lira a month The State paid Ida a pension when Mussolini was on war service and when he was wounded by a mortar shell, the police notified her that her husband had been wounded in action.

The marriage between Mussolini and Rachele had had a devastating effect on Ida. She claimed to be his wife and invaded Rachele's apartments. Once he was in power, he took steps to remove evidence of their relationship, though the records ordering payment of the maintenance for Benito were overlooked. Ida made a nuisance of herself, bringing her son to Milan, making noisy scenes in the offices of *Il Popolo* or in cafes.[212] She claimed that he had promised to marry her, that he was a traitor and that he had accepted a bribe from the French Government during the war to campaign for Italy to join the Allied powers. Eventually Mussolini had had enough and, in 1926, he had her confined to a lunatic asylum. She ended up on the Island of San Clemente in Venice, where she died in 1937. Benito was equally badly treated. He was the subject of surveillance by the authorities but continued to repeat that Mussolini was his father. Eventually, he was confined to an asylum in the Province of Milan and, in August 1942, he died from a series of coma-inducing injections.[213]

Margherita Sarfatti was Mussolini's mistress from 1911 and remained so off and on, until 1938 when, because of her Jewish ancestry, she left Italy and went to live in the Argentine. Margherita had been born in Venice in 1880. Her father was a wealthy lawyer in Venice and she was brought up in a palazzo and privately educated. Attracted by socialist ideas, she left home at the age of 18 and married a lawyer from Padua, some 13 years older than her. She was not only well educated but something of an intellectual who was an art critic for *Avanti*. As a journalist she was much involved in the cultural shaping of Italian art. In 1911, she met Mussolini, became his mistress and had considerable influence in furthering the fascist cause, particularly in the United States,

212 Monelli p 89.
213 *The Times*, 13 January 2005

where she played an important part in selling Mussolini to the American people.

She not only edited his magazine *Gerarchia Butalso* but, in 1925, she wrote the first official biography of Mussolini. After she had been displaced in his life by others, Mussolini confessed that the book was ridiculous rubbish, and only published because he knew that invention was more useful than the truth.[214] Ida Dalser gets no mention. By 1934 he had broken with Margherita completely.[215] Mussolini adopted the German laws about Jews, who hitherto had enjoyed freedom in Italy from anti-semitism. As a result, in 1938, Margherita left Italy, having in any event now been replaced by Carla Petacci in Mussolini's favours. Margherita went to live in the Argentine and Uruguay, only returning to Italy after the war. She continued to be an influential force in Italian art. Her view of Mussolini was one of idolatry. She described him in this passage from her biography "Then he went on:—And yet— and yet! Yes, I am obsessed by this wild desire—it consumes my whole being. I want to make a mark on my era with my will, like a lion with its claw! A mark like this!" And as with a claw, he scratched the cover of a chair-back from end to end!" She died in 1961.

Clara Petacci was born in February 1912 and died with Mussolini in April 1945. His love affair with her, which was at first a real passion, was very different from his other love affairs, and gave to the last hours of his life a saving romance and pathos.[216] Their relationship started properly in 1936, though they had known each other for some four years before. She had been infatuated with him since she was a child. By the autumn of 1936, when she was separated from her husband, she became his favoured mistress. The meetings in the Palazzo were romantic. They sat on marble. He telephoned her every day, sometime talking sentimentally about swallows and poetry. Mussolini confided in her that the thought of her had kept him awake all night.

---

214 Mack Smith p125
215 Kirkpatrick p 176
216 Monelli p 142

She was installed in his private apartment in the Palazzo Venezia. She was ardent, young, and submissive. She was described as being pretty with curly black hair and grey-green eyes. Her photos do not do full justice to her. Her youth and gaiety endeared her to him and he needed to see her every day and several times a day. When he was making speeches, he insisted that she came to watch so that he could see her. She tried to give him advice, but he wanted to hold the floor. He seems not to have been particularly generous to her, though she was able to get credit from tradesmen because of the Mussolini connection. They behaved like a married couple, though often living apart. Because of her position, she spent a good deal of time answering correspondence from the public who were asking for help, and money and making complaints about injustices.

His biographer described the position: "During those crowded and fateful years between 1916 and 1940, the biographer seems to be dealing with two different people. One is a middle aged man, made soft by the love of a simple and affectionate woman, for whom he would keep important visitors waiting. He would indulge in youthful escapades, and interrupt conferences in Munich or Berlin to telephone trite messages of love. The other figure is the Dictator, obsessed with the idea of conquests and wars, always in military dress, ordering military reviews, — regimenting the whole country, including the children, in the dreary discipline of fascist uniform and parades."[217] In the summer of 1942, they had spent a happy time at the coast, managing to escape from his family. He was, by this time, suffering from illness and pain. His memory was failing and in three months he lost twenty kilograms. When he attended meetings, he looked almost moribund.[218].

In 1943, Clara suffered from a severe attack of peritonitis and Mussolini was constantly at her bedside. She began to worry about being replaced by younger rivals. Their relationship was now public knowledge and there were times when he thought of

217 Ibid p 164
218 Mack Smith p 285

getting rid of her. In May, he had her stopped at the entrance to the Palazzio, but after tears and entreaties, she was reinstated. Her anxieties remained. Again, he tried to stop her visits but was unsuccessful. Their relationship now altered and on one occasion she found her photo torn into pieces. She went to live on Lake Gardone, where she was a virtual prisoner. In April 1945, Mussolini went to Milan and was reunited with Carla. They decided to see whether they could get to Switzerland but were captured by partisans. Carla had the opportunity to escape but loyally stayed with Mussolini. On 28 April he and she were shot, and next day their bodies were hung upside down in front of a petrol station. The prey remained faithful to the predator.

CHAPTER SIXTEEN

HAROLD LASKI

While it is usually great men (or women) who are affected by the aphrodisiac of power, it is not a universal truism. Little men like (Northcliffe and Rothermere) who can have delusions of grandeur and an exaggerated belief in their own power are no less susceptible to the same aphrodisiac. Such a man was Harold Laski, whose hapless behaviour towards Churchill and Attlee in 1945, brought him, for the first time to the attention of a bemused public and to subsequent humiliation. In May 1945, the war against Germany which had started in 1939 had ended. From the spring of 1940, the Government of which Churchill had been Prime Minister and Attlee, the Labour party leader, his deputy, had been run by a War Cabinet as a coalition of different parties and individuals. The war against Japan had still to be won and in 1945 no immediate prospect of success appeared to be in sight. In those circumstances, the question arose as to whether the coalition should continue or whether the parties should go their own way. Churchill wished the coalition to continue but, on 21 May the Labour party voted against staying in. Churchill formed a caretaker Conservative government. Thereafter there was election fever with ever increasing animosity between the parties. Into this cauldron of bitterness came the unlikely figure of Harold Laski to stoke the embers.

Laski had been born in 1893.He was educated at Manchester Grammar school and at New College, Oxford. Thereafter, he led a distinguished academic life and in 1926 became Professor of Political Science at The London School of Economics, He was a prolific writer and a brilliant lecturer both in England and the

United States. He became a proponent of Marxism and in 1932 joined the Socialist League, a left wing faction outside the control of the Labour Party. The Socialist League was dissolved in 1937 and, thereafter, Laski became a member of the Labour Party's National Executive Committee (NEC.) By 1944, he had become chairman of the Party Conference and was Chairman of the Party from 1945-1946. This latter was a post given without election, to the longest serving member of the NEC who had not held it before. It was in the latter capacity that he was to cross swords with Attlee which was, in the end, to be his undoing.

Attlee had been educated at Haileybury College and at University College, Oxford where he got a second class degree. His father who was a solicitor encouraged Attlee to go to the Bar but it was a visit to the Stepney Boys' Club in 1905 that was to have a significant impact on his life. He left the Bar and took up social work in the East End. In due course he became manager of the Club and Secretary of Toynbee Hall. He joined the Independent Labour Party, campaigned against The Poor Law, stood twice for the Stepney Borough Council and twice for the Limehouse Board of Guardians. In 1912, he became a lecturer on Local Government at the London School of Economics and in particular dealt with students about to go into social work.

In 1915, he fought in Gallipoli and later was in charge of the rearguard during the evacuation. From there he went to serve in Mesopotamia where he was wounded. He did two tours of France where in 1918 he was again wounded and returned to England. Thereafter he involved himself in local politics, becoming Mayor of Stepney at the young age of 36. In November 1922, he was elected MP for Limehouse. At the General Election in 1929, Labour became the largest party with Macdonald as Prime Minister. But in 1931, Macdonald formed a National Government (including some Labour members but not all) because of the financial crisis which Baldwin subsequently transformed into a Conservative government. It left Labour supporters accusing Macdonald of being a traitor, echoes of which can still be heard today. Henderson succeeded Macdonald as Labour leader, followed soon afterwards by George Lansbury. Attlee in turn succeeded Lansbury as Leader in 1935 in rather dramatic circumstances.

The Labour Party Conference in 1935 took place in the shadow of Italy's pending invasion of Abyssinia. Debate centred on the question of imposing sanctions. Lansbury, a well-known pacifist, said: "I believe that force never has and never will bring permanent peace and goodwill in the world. God intends us to live peacefully and quietly with one another. If some people do not allow us to do so, I am ready to stand as the early Christians did and say this is our faith, this is here we stand and, if necessary, this is where we will die."[219] Bevin, the very robust General Secretary of the Transport and General Workers Union was incensed and said: "It is placing the Executive and the Movement in an absolutely wrong position to be hawking your conscience around from body to body, asking to be told what to do with it."[220] The anti-war motion was lost and Lansbury resigned. Attlee thus became leader of the Labour Party, a position which he was to hold for another 20 years.

In 1940, Laski was to act as one of Attlee's unofficial advisors. He had earlier expressed the view that "he (Attlee) hasn't got an ounce of leadership in him."[221] In 1943 he described Attlee as "uninspiring and uninteresting."[222] Throughout the war, Laski produced a series of papers particularly on domestic reform and war aims. Attlee's attitude was that these were matters to dealt with when the war had been won and told Laski so. It did little to stop the outflow. Matters came to a head in February 1942, when Churchill reshuffled his Government and sacked Greenwood, the Labour Minister who was in charge of post war reconstruction. Laski sought to engage the NEC in an unsuccessful attempt to remove Attlee as the leader of the Labour party. In a memorandum

---

219 Labour Party. *Report of the 35th Annual Conference* (London. Labour Party 1935)p 175
220 Ibid p 178
221 Newman, Michael. *Harold Laski. A Political Biography* (Macmillan Press. Ltd. Basingstoke Hampshire. 1993) p 211
222 Ibid p 246

to the NEC, he urged adoption of a socialist policy even if it were to lead to the break-up of the coalition. The public expression of these thoughts brought him a reprimand from the NEC. Further his desire for a closer relationship with progressive forces abroad (i.e. the Communists) found little favour with the Labour leadership.

After the start of the election in May 1945, Laski wrote to Attlee: "I have been acutely aware for many months—of the strong feeling that the continuance of your leadership in the party is a grave handicap to our hopes of victory in the coming election" He then cited the similar views of the NEC executive, the outstanding trade union leaders, the candidates, the rank and file and parliamentary colleagues. He ended the letter "your resignation of the leadership now would be a great service to the Party."[223] Attlee took no notice.

Churchill was due to go to Potsdam together with Truman (Roosevelt's successor) to meet Stalin to discuss Peace Terms. He offered Attlee access to foreign policy papers and, on 2 June, he invited Attlee to join him so as to present a joint front. Having consulted colleagues but not the NEC, Attlee accepted. Laski, suspicious of Attlee, was determined to assert his authority as chairman of the Party. He wrote to Attlee: "I assume that you will take steps to make it clear that neither you nor the Party can be regarded as bound by any decisions taken at the meeting and that you can be present for information and consultation only————if you do not share my view I think I must, as chairman, call a special meeting of the Executive Committee to consider the point. This is far too grave a matter to settle without discussion."[224] Laski continued to express the same view publicly, but Attlee rejected his views.

On 26 July, when the results of the election were announced, Laski wrote another letter to Attlee suggesting that he should refuse to form a government until the new MPs had met and made their choice of who was to be their leader. Attlee replied: "I thank you for your letter, the contents of which have been noted."

223 H.Laski .Correspondence. History Archive, Manchester. LP/LAS/38/21/ii
224 Ibid LP/LAS/38/20

Morrison (a leading Labour Minister) tried to persuade Attlee not to go to the Palace (where the King was waiting to invite him to become Prime Minister), until the Parliamentary Party had met and decided on their choice of leader. Attlee ignored them both. He went to the Palace, saw the King and returned as Prime Minister, to the discomfort of both Laski and Morrison.

Further problems arose because, after the election victory, Laski persisted in claiming, in a number of public pronouncements, that the Labour Government would follow a socialist foreign policy. He was determined to use his position as Party Chairman to dictate to the Government what their strategy should be on this issue. Eventually the taciturn Attlee could stand it no longer. He wrote to Laski "You have no right whatever to speak on behalf of the Government. Foreign affairs are in the capable hands of Ernest Bevin. His task is quite sufficiently difficult without the embarrassment of irresponsible statements of the kind you are making—I can assure you that there is widespread resentment in the Party at your activities and a period of silence on your part would be welcome."[225] Laski's proposal that he should be found some job in the embassy in Washington because: "he knew America with a quite special intimacy and had a great many friends all over the country", fell on equally deaf ears. [226] He was offered no post in Attlee's administration and gradually his prestige and influence decreased.

The final damage to his reputation was his unsuccessful libel action which arose from what he was alleged to have said at an election meeting at Newark on 16 June 1945. At the meeting, Wentworth Day, who was a political adviser to the Conservative candidate, deliberately provoked Laski. Laski was reported as saying: "If we cannot get the reforms we desire we shall not hesitate to use violence." The exact words used (which included references to "revolution") and their interpretation were the

225 Butler, David and Butler, Gareth. *Twentieth Century British Political Facts.* (Palgrave Macmillan. London. 2005) p 289
226 Williams, Francis. *A Prime Minister Remembers.* (William Heinemann Ltd. London.1961) p 7

subject of much debate at the libel trial which took place in 1947 before Lord Goddard, Lord Chief Justice and a special jury. Sir Patrick Hastings K.C who had been Attorney General in Ramsay Macdonald's Labour Government in 1924, appeared for the defendant newspapers and subjected Laski to a powerful cross examination in which Laski was made to look helpless and shifty. The jury took only forty minutes to return a verdict that the newspaper article was fair and accurate. Laski took his defeat badly. While Attlee went on to preside over what most commentators still regard as one of the great administrations of the century, Laski became seriously depressed and ceased to be a force in the ideological battles within the Labour Party. He died in March 1950. Thus the pragmatic prey triumphed over the intellectual predator.

CHAPTER SEVENTEEN

KING EDWARD VIII, MRS SIMPSON AND OTHERS

It is difficult to know, in the familiar love story of the King and his mistress, Mrs Simpson, who was the predator and who was the prey. The romantic story which gripped the world in 1935 and 1936, ended, as so many golden occasions do, in something akin to farce. A journalist summed it up when he wrote: "Denied dignity, and without anything useful to do, the new Duke of Windsor and his Duchess would be international society's most notorious parasites for a generation, while they thoroughly bored each other—She had thought of him as emotionally a Peter Pan, and of herself as an Alice in Wonderland. The book they had written together, however was a Paradise lost."[227] She summed up her life "You have no idea how hard it is to live out a great romance." How was it then that the marriage of the glamorous young Prince of Wales and the equally attractive young divorcee from Baltimore proved to be so lacking in substance? She was not his only mistress. There were others with whom he was in love; Marion Coke, Portia Cadogan, Rosemary Leveson-Gower and Thelma Furness are the best known. But his main affair was with Freda Dudley Ward which lasted from 1918 until she was replaced first by Thelma Furness, and then by Mrs Simpson in 1935. However, before them all was an affair with Marguerite Alibert, *demi-mondaine* and courtesan, who in 1923 was charged with the murder of her husband, Prince Ali Fahmy.

---

227 *Washington Post* 8 June 1986

Edward (often known as David) was born in 1894. His great grandmother, Queen Victoria had been on the throne for some 57 years and it would be another seven years before she died and was succeeded by King Edward VII. Edward's father, later King George V, had married his dead brother's fiancée, Princess Mary of Teck. Edward's parents were somewhat narrow minded. George had served as a naval officer and his horizons were limited. His chief interest was stamp collecting. It was decided that Edward should, after a period of private tuition, join the Navy. He managed to pass the exam for the Naval College at Osborne on the Isle of Wight and so, in May 1907, at the age of 13, he became a cadet there. He seems to have grown up and was now much more able to look after himself.[228] From Osborne, Edward moved to the Royal Naval College at Dartmouth in 1909. His life was substantially altered when in 1910, his grandfather Edward VII died and his mother and father became King and Queen. He himself was now the Prince of Wales.

After a short period, serving as a midshipman in HMS Hindustan, it was decided that he should go up to Magdalen College, Oxford. He seems to have enjoyed the social and sporting life at Oxford but he found the academic work difficult and boring and decided to come down before taking a degree. He started on a ferocious social round as a preliminary to serving for a few years in the Army. The outbreak of War in August 1914 altered the Prince's plans as it did millions of others. He was enabled to join the Grenadier Guards but had to remain in England, becoming involved in some Patriotic Fund raising. Eventually, he was allowed to join the staff of Sir John French, C in C of the BEF. But he complained that he was kept well away from the front and was not well occupied.[229] When, occasionally, he was allowed to go near the front, he still regarded his presence in France as something of a waste of time. The award of an MC and promotion to Captain he regarded with distaste, as he knew he had not been involved in the fighting and that there were many other officers who deserved the award.

---

228 Ziegler, Philip. *King Edward VIII* (William Collins, Sons & Co Ltd. London.1990) p 23
229 Ibid p54.

Finding France most uncongenial, he accepted the idea of a tour of the Middle East with alacrity. Here, for the first time, he experienced the adulation of the troops that was so often to be his lot over the next twenty years.[230] After a short return to France, he found himself on the Italian front, from where he again returned to France to visit Canadian troops and, after the Armistice, Australian and American troops. His view about the effect of the war on him was summed up in a speech he made in May 1919 when he received the freedom of the City of London: "The part I played was, I fear, a very insignificant one, but from one point of view I shall never forget my periods of service overseas. In those four years, I mixed with men. In those four years, I found my manhood. When I think of the future, and the heavy responsibilities which may fall to my lot, I feel the experience gained since 1914 will stand me in good stead."[231]

He first met Marguerite Alibert in April 1917, at 20 Rue Bizet, one of the "grandest maison de rendezvous" in wartime Paris. During 1917 and 1918, he wrote a whole series of indiscreet love letters to her, but the relationship was soon to come to an end, no doubt, he hoped, without serious consequences. In 1918, she tried blackmailing him. In 1923, when she was charged with murder, it is suggested that most of his letters were recovered in exchange for the establishment concealing her previous reputation at her trial.[232]

But before that there had been two short love affairs. The first was with Marion Coke, the wife of Viscount Coke and next with Portia Cadogan. Of her, Asquith wrote in 1915: "as among the younger women about the Court, the only one to catch the eye, even for a moment, was Portia Cadogan."[233] Edward wrote frequent passionate letters to them both.[234] Rosemary

230 Ibid p 71
231 Speeches by H.R.H. The Prince of Wales 1912-1926 London 1927)
232 Rose, Andrew. *The Prince, The Princess and the Perfect Murder.* (Coronet, London 2013) passim
233 Brock, Michael and Eleanor Brock. *H.H.Asquith .Letters to Venetia Stanley.*(Oxford University Press, Oxford 1982) p 540
234 Ziegler pp 90-93

Levenson-Gower was another of Edward's favourites, though there appears to have been no romance. Cynthia Asquith recorded: "So far he (Prince of Wales) dances most with Rosemary and also motors with her in the daytime."[235] She was disquietingly attractive, which appealed to Duff Cooper, whose attempts at an affair seem to have been unproductive. "I had a long talk with her and told her I loved her. She said I mustn't—that she was very fond of me but could not be in love with me"[236]

Edward had had a long time relationship with Freda Dudley Ward. He had first met her in February 1918, and it was not until mid 1934 that it came to an end in a somewhat brutal way. They first met when Edward was at a dance in Belgrave Square and Freda and her escort were taking shelter in the doorway because of an air raid warning. They were invited in and Edward danced with her for the rest of the evening.[237] They were both aged 23. She had been married for five years to a man 16 years older than herself. He was a Liberal MP. It was an amiable formality and they both led separate lives. Immediately after meeting at the dance, Edward wrote to her asking to see her. By mistake, the letter was opened by her mother in law who invited him to tea. The affair began at once and they were soon writing passionate love letters to each other. In all, he wrote some three thousand letters to her. When, in 1919, he was due to go to Canada, he tried unsuccessfully to persuade her to go with him. He found his tour of Commonwealth Countries, without her, depressing. For four or five years until 1923 it is clear that he was madly in love with her and she with him. His love continued until the arrival of Thelma.

Freda was variously described as small, elegant and exceptionally pretty. Lady Loughborough described her as "absolutely fascinating to look at; she had a good mind; a tremendous character, great loyalty and a wonderful sense of humour. She built one up and made one feel amusing and attractive. She had a strong

235 Asquith, Lady Cynthia, *Diaries 1915-1918* (Century. London 1968) pp116-117
236 Norwich, John Julius (ed) *The Duff Cooper Diaries 1915-1951*(Phoenix, London 2006) pp 44 & 63
237 Ziegler p94

influence on us all." Photographs of her at the time do not do justice to that description. She had an independence of mind, was a good golfer, and tennis player as well as being an accomplished dancer. Her father was a lace manufacturer from Nottingham.

From 1923, Edward and Freda maintained a relationship but at a less hectic pace. She was undoubtedly having an affair with Michael Herbert and was contemplating divorcing her husband, though they remained married until 1931. However she continued as a confidante to Edward. In that role, she played an important part in keeping him from being depressed. He wrote to her at this time: "My God it's damn silly that you and I aren't married, my angel—Anyway we love each other, nothing can change that."[238] He kept in touch with her but Thelma's arrival spelt trouble and when Wallis appeared on the scene, Freda's reign was at an end. After her divorce from Dudley Ward she married the Marques de Casa Maury in 1937. They were divorced in 1954.

From the very beginning he had written passionate letters to Freda. The day after being invited to tea, he wrote "Dear Mrs Ward" and suggesting further meetings. There were two further letters on 7/8 March, 1918, making arrangements to meet and, by 26 March, he was addressing her as "My Angel". The letter ended "Again thank you, millions & millions& Millions of times for everything my angel; tons & tons of love from your E."[239] He continued in the same vein, writing to her at least once a day and on one day in August 1922, apart from telephoning her, he wrote to her three times.[240]

Some idea of the nature of their friendship can be gathered from the letters. He was full of self-pity about the misery of being Prince of Wales, of the tiresome formalities of Court, of a boring and unrewarding routine and of the frustration of being separated from the woman he so adored and who provided him with the

---

238 Ibid p174.
239 Godfrey, Rupert.(ed) *Letters from a Prince.* (Winner Books, London.1999)
     pp 9 & 11
240 Ziegler p 95

strength to face up to the problems inherent in his position as Prince of Wales. There is no doubt, however, that by the middle of the 1920s her ardour had waned somewhat, though she continued to remain the recipient of his confidences, and a sympathetic listener to his outpourings. By that time she had recognised that, as a love affair, it had no future from her point of view (nor indeed from his), though like all love affairs it had its ups and downs. Some hint of her anxiety about the relationship can be found in a letter which Freda wrote as early as June 1920. Edward described her letter: "I've got the gist of it, that we must make the greatest sacrifice of our lives & give up our LOVE!!" He also added: "Whatever might happen Freddie darling you'll always know that your poor worn out little David, so entirely faithful and devoted to his precious sacred blessed divine little goddess & idol his Freddie whom he loves & adores & worships as no man has ever loved adored or worshipped before or ever will again!!"[241]

A picture of his life emerges from the letters On 10 September, 1918, he had written from France: "You know darling girl that you've changed my whole life & way of looking at things; it all seems so different since last leave in England—I feel older somehow, but much happier, though as you know I get fearful fits of depression."[242] His trips abroad merely exacerbated his dislike of Royal protocol and official engagements. In September 1919, while in Canada, he wrote: "I really am down and out tonight sweetheart & feeling like death, as I've never taken such a hopelessly miserable, despondent view of life as I do now! It's hell, beloved one, & all on account of having the P of W stunt & play to the gallery until I can do it no more!!—I feel I'm through, & realise as I have so often told, you sweetheart that I'm not ½ big enough to take on what I consider is about the biggest job in the world!!"[243]

Freda's friendship with Michael Herbert may have played some part in her gradual withdrawal from her intense relationship

---

241 Letters p410
242 Ibid p 97
243 Ibid p232

with Edward. He was the younger brother of the Earl of Pembroke. He was described by Edward as: "being dangerous, not to be trusted, and not a fit friend for Freda, someone whom he loathed with a hatred that passeth all understanding."[244] By September 1923, Freda had obviously tired of the love affair with Edward and told him so. He replied: "I can't help hating and loathing the fact that you are in love with somebody and it was a big blow when you told me the other day. It's a horrid thought for me that I really mean nothing whatever to you now though you mean the hell of a lot to me, bless you."[245] Though they remained very close friends, the relationship now assumed that of two old friends. In 1929 he was to write: "I know our two lives aren't absolutely satisfactory and I'm afraid they won't ever be now, but I do know this, my angel, that I love you too much to ever be able to love anyone else ever again. I'm always comparing and they can't any of them compare and I'm so glad, I lost my head once over a crazy physical attraction. Look at the result. Just made a fool of myself, that's all. Nothing left of it but nausea."[246]

Eventually her position was usurped by Thelma, and then by Wallis. In 1934, when Freda rang to speak to Edward, she was told by the operator that instructions had been left that she was not to be put through. She died aged 88 in 1953. She kept silent about her relationship with Edward. Her tact and discretion were part of her make up.

Thelma was described as "exquisitely pretty, glossy, elegant, good natured and relentlessly frivolous." She was born in 1904 in Switzerland, the daughter of an American Diplomat. At the age of 17 she was married for the first time and divorced some three years later. In 1926 she married Viscount Furness, the Chairman of Furness Shipping Company. In the same year she had met Edward at a dance at Londonderry House, but it was not until June 1929 that they met again. The occasion was the Leicestershire Agricultural Show at Leicester. Edward invited her to dine with him and thereafter they met regularly. In early 1930, Edward went

244 Ibid pp161,313 & 333
245 Ziegler p 101
246 Ibid p102

on safari in East Africa where Thelma and her husband joined him. The relationship rapidly developed and she was his constant companion. In 1934, she went to visit her sister in America, suggesting to Wallis that: "she should look after him while I'm away. See that he doesn't get into mischief". Wallis did not allow the opportunity to pass and Thelma ceased to be a favourite. When Edward's memoirs (*A King's Story*) came to be published in 1951, both Freda and Thelma's names were noticeably absent.

Wallis Simpson was born in Pennsylvania on 19 June 1896. She was the only child of Teakle and Alice Warfield. Her father died when she was a few months old. As a child, she and her mother were dependent on the charity of relations and they were constantly moving house. Two of the influences on life was her grandmother and her uncle, Sol. Her grandmother had an implacable hatred of Yankees and one of her favourite sayings was "Never marry a Yankee." Wallis described Uncle Sol: "For a long and impressionable period he was the nearest thing to a father in my silent, uncertain world." [247] He was a banker of means, President of the Continental Trust Company and an entrepreneur. In 1908 her mother remarried, though in 1913 once again she was widowed. In 1912, through the benevolence of another uncle, Wallis went to an expensive girls' school in Maryland. There she appears to have been a hardworking and industrious student. In those days girls when they left school did not go on to college because "the only purpose of a sedate and well-regulated school was to prepare a girl for the marriage market."[248]

It is perhaps surprising that she achieved three husbands despite this description of herself: "My endowments were definitely on the scanty side. Nobody ever called me beautiful or even pretty. I was thin in an era when a certain plumpness was a girl's ideal. My jaw was clearly too big and too pointed to be classic. My hair was straight where the laws of compensation might at least have provided curls.—No one has ever accused me

---

247 Windsor, Duchess of. *The Heart has its Reasons*.(Chivers Press, Bath.1983) p 21.
248 Ibid p 50

of being an intellectual,"[249] But what made her such a formidable predator was ruthless ambition, based no doubt on a determination to avenge early struggles and to secure, against competition, someone else's man. "In society she was ruthless and voracious, the fact that a boy belonged to some other girl was a challenge in itself." [250]

In April 1916, on a visit to her cousin, she met Lieutenant Earl Winfield Spenser, (known as Win) a naval aviator at the air base at Pensacola, Florida. He was ten years older than her, quiet, soft spoken, and taciturn. Unfortunately he was also an alcoholic. Their marriage gradually fell apart. He was depressed at lack of promotion. He took to drink, which intensified his jealous and sadistic streak. There were separations and reconciliations but by 1925 they were permanently living apart. In December 1927, they were divorced. By this time she had met Ernest Simpson and, after his marriage was dissolved in July 1928, they were married. He had an English father and American mother. He was a former officer in the Coldstream Guards and an Anglo-American Shipping Executive. They set up home in London. Although Wallis lost all her investments in the Wall Street crash in 1929, the shipping business prospered and Wallis and Ernest led a very comfortable life in London. Matters were to change when she met Edward.

It is strange that such an event should give rise to doubt about its date. She thinks it was in the fall of 1930 while he is sure it was in the winter of 1931. Ziegler suggests 10 January 1931.[251] Thereafter they were to meet on infrequent occasions. He would visit Bryanston Court where the Simpsons lived and she stayed at Fort Belvedere, Edward's place in Windsor Great Park. As early as August 1933, the Duchess of York was writing to Queen Mary "A certain person (Mrs Simpson) had been at the Fort—relations are already a little difficult when naughty ladies are brought in

---

249 *The Heart.* pp 13/14
250 Ziegler p 225
251 *The Heart* p165.*A King's Story.* p 254. Ziegler p 227.

and up to now we have not met "the lady" at all,& I would like to remain quite outside the whole affair."[252]

But it was in January 1934, when Thelma sailed to the United States that left the field open for Wallis. Shortly after Freda had been given her marching orders, Wallis took charge of Edward's domestic life. In August 1934, they were together on a holiday at Biarritz and then a cruise on a yacht ending up, after a storm, at Cannes. There, Edward produced a tiny velvet case containing a diamond and emerald charm for Wallis' bracelet. In February 1935, he again went on holiday with a party which included Wallis, to Kitzbuhel. By this time Ernest had had enough of the Prince, declined to join the party and took himself off to New York. When he and Wallis were reunited in England, the marriage was effectively over.

Meanwhile Edward and Wallis continued their relationship, much to the chagrin of their courtiers and the disapproval of his family. It was a relationship of which society were now aware though not yet a matter of speculation in the press, at any rate in the English press. Again, they went away on holiday together to the south of France, followed by a cruise in the Mediterranean. From there, they went on to Budapest and Vienna, not returning until October. They spent New Year together, at a fancy dress ball, but Edward was not to remain Prince of Wales for long because, on 20 January 1936, King George V died and Edward became King. What was their relationship at this time? It was her personality, not her appearance, which captivated him. Unlike other women, she treated him like a child and dominated him. She soon realised, whatever the future held by way of marriage, that when he became king, it was vital not to lose hold of his affection for her. There can be no doubt that his affection for her far outweighed hers for him. "Total devotion it certainly was, slavish devotion, some would say but he found contentment in it".[253]

---

252 Shawcross, William(Ed) *Counting Our Blessings*. (Macmillan. London 2012) p 199
253 Ziegler p 237

In May, he told her that he was inviting Baldwin, now Prime Minister to dinner with her: "Sooner or later he must meet my future wife."[254] In January 1936, Duff Cooper recorded: "I think she is a nice woman and a sensible woman.—but she is as hard as nails and she doesn't love him." [255].

The presence of Wallis at dinner parties and holidays with Edward were duly recorded in the Court Circular but the British press, although well aware of the articles in the American and other foreign papers, kept a discreet silence on the subject. The announcement that Wallis was to take divorce proceedings in October led to frenzied speculation about the prospects of her marrying Edward, but none of this reached the British public. Edward subsequently described how, with the help of Walter Monckton K.C., he enlisted the aid of Lord Rothermere, pro-prietor of both *The Daily Mail* and *The Evening News* and Lord Beaverbrook, the proprietor of both *The Daily Express* and *The Evening Standard*. "At my request Max Beaverbrook came to the Palace—I told him frankly of my problem—my one desire was to protect Wallis from sensational publicity, at least in my own country—Max heard me out—Without delay he began a prodigious task—he achieved the miracle I desired—" a gentlemen's agreement" among newspapers to report the case without sensation."[256] Shortly thereafter Baldwin met Edward and tried to persuade him to get Wallis to drop her divorce petition. He declined. In November, Baldwin went to the Palace. There, Edward told him about his attitude towards Mrs Simson: "I want you to know that I have made up my mind and that nothing will alter it. I have looked at it from all sides and I mean to abdicate to marry Mrs Simpson."[257]

Constitutionally there was no prospect of them marrying while he was King. The Cabinet and the Dominions were against

---

254 *The Heart* p 225
255 Norwich, John Julius. (Ed) *The Duff Cooper Diaries*.(Phoenix, London 2006) p228
256 *A King's Story* p315
257 Hyde, H. Montgomery. *Walter Monckton*. (Sinclair-Stevenson.Ltd. London.1991) p 53

it. Because of the increasing public drama, Wallis was persuaded to go abroad from where she issued a statement: "Mrs Simpson, throughout the last few weeks has invariably wished to avoid any action or proposal which would hurt or damage His Majesty or the Throne. Today her attitude is unchanged, and she is willing, if such action would solve the problem, to withdraw forthwith from a situation that has been rendered both unhappy and untenable." When they next spoke on the phone Edward made it clear that he would not give her up: "You can go wherever you want—to China, Labrador, or the South Seas. But wherever you go, I will follow"[258] In his final address to the Nation, he made it clear that Wallis had tried up to the last to persuade him to take a different course.[259] He abdicated on 11 December and it was to France, and then Vienna, that he was to go. Though they telephoned each other regularly, because of the divorce laws they could not live together until her decree was made absolute in May. Finally on June 3, they were married in France.

Not only did the Court make it clear that Wallis was to be ignored, but also that she was not even to be accorded the title of Her Royal Highness. Thus, he was now to be called His Royal Highness the Duke of Windsor; she was simply to have the title of Duchess. It was made obvious that her presence in England would be unwelcome and it was to be many years before she again set foot in this country. Edward wrote angry letters to the King about the members of his family. In particular, he was angry with his mother, Queen Mary, who did not send a wedding present: "I am bitterly hurt and disappointed that you ignored the most important event of my life—You must realise by this time that as there is a limit to what one's feelings can endure, this most unjust and uncalled for treatment can have but one important result; my complete estrangement from all of you."[260] No members of the Royal Family attended the wedding. The Dukes of Kent and Gloucester sent presents. The Duke of Kent's present of a Faberge

---

258 *A King's Story* pp 397 & 403
259 Ibid p 413
260 Ziegler pp 360 & 361

Egg was returned. The Queen sent some cutlery. The Duchess was to write: "only one thing marred our happiness; after the first burst of joy in rediscovering each other and being together, we found our minds turning back in interminable post-mortems concerning the events leading up to the Abdication.—we vowed we never would discuss the Abdication again, and to this day we never have."[261].

In October 1937, they paid a visit to Germany where they met the leading Nazis and had tea with Hitler at Berchestgaden, which gave rise to suggestions that they had some sympathy with the regime. They continued to live in France, but Edward was obsessed by his remoteness from political events and by a desire to return to England with the Duchess. Monckton tried to persuade the King, not only to receive Edward, but also, to find some job for him. But the King was against a visit at that time and the Queen was against giving Edward any role.[262] In July 1938, the King and Queen paid a state visit to France and the Windsors prudently removed themselves from Paris. When Edward met the Prime Minister, Chamberlain, he made it clear that any return to Britain before early summer of 1939 was out of the question. In the result, the outbreak of war in September 1939, effectively put an end to the immediate question.

When war broke out the Government made it clear that, if the Windsors were to return to England, Edward must either become Deputy Regional Commissioner for Wales or act as Liaison Officer with the British Military Mission. He chose the latter post and he and Wallis now returned to England, but apart from one short visit by Edward to see the King, they were ignored by other members of the Royal Family. Their attitude was summed up in a letter which the Queen wrote to Queen Mary in September 1939: "I haven't heard a word about Mrs Simpson. I trust that she will soon return to France and STAY THERE. I am sure she hates this dear country, & therefore she should not be here in wartime".[263]

---

261 *The Heart*, pp 299 & 300
262 Shawcross p 94
263 Ibid p 279

Edward's post was now changed to be part of the British Mission to the French Commander in Chief. There he remained until the Germans occupied France in May 1940 and the Windsors took themselves off, first to Spain and then to Portugal. The question of his future employment now arose.

In the event he was offered the Governorship of the Bahamas. Wallis' reaction was that the "proposal was anything but welcomed and was in fact heart-breaking for both of us." However her view changed after being there and a chapter in her book is headed *Nassau Five Fruitful Years*.[264] There she threw herself into the role of the Governor's wife, working for the Red Cross, organising clinics, improving infant welfare and setting up a club for the troops now pouring into the island after America entered the war. She took on various social duties and raised funds for the war effort. The war bypassed the Bahamas and the Windsors were anxious to play a role on a bigger stage. In May 1945, after the end of the war against Germany, they left the Bahamas and, in September, returned to France. In October, Edward went to England and had a successful visit with the King and with Queen Mary. The door however was still shut to his coming to live in England permanently. A suggestion that he might find some official position in Washington came to nothing.

While there were many comments about how happy they appeared to be with each other, not everyone agreed. Diana Cooper, an old friend and now the Ambassador's wife in Paris, wrote in September 1945: "The two poor little old things were most pathetic. Fear, I suppose, of losing their youthful figures, or home sickness, has made them Dachau-thin. She is much commoner and more confident, he much duller and sillier." Diana did not imagine that the Duke found Wallis any more congenial than she him: "He saw her, she felt, as a sort of Folle de Chaillot." (The mad woman of Chaillot rescued the city from corrupt business men.) It can't be helped, we do very badly together."[265]

---

264 *The Heart* p344
265 Ziegler, Philip. *Diana Cooper* (Penguin Books. Harmondsworth. Middlesex.1983) p 278

Duff Cooper described one aspect of Edward's life in an entry in his diary for 14 March 1946. He wrote: "The Duke of Windsor came to see me this morning at his own request. I thought he wanted to consult me about something—but not at all. He sat here for nearly an hour, chattering about one thing and another. I expect the truth is that he is so desoeuvre that Wallis, to get him out of the house, said "why don't you go round to see Duff one morning and have an interesting talk about politics."[266] Duff Cooper's views on Wallis were no more charitable. On June 7 1946, he wrote in his diary: "Wallis was looking strikingly plain. It is sad to think that he gave up the position of King Emperor not to live in an island of the Hesperides with the Queen of Beauty but to share an apartment on the third floor of the Ritz with this harsh-voiced ageing woman who was never even very pretty."[267] In July 1948, "he thought the Windsors looked faded and worn."[268]

Thereafter they settled down to a dull life in France. They were still effectively discouraged from visits to England. The Queen wrote in 1951: "You can imagine that I do not want to see the Duke of Windsor—the part author of the King's troubles".[269] They were not invited to the wedding of Princess Elizabeth and Prince Philip. Further attempts to get Wallis a Royal Title continued to fall on deaf ears at the Court. The Duke had no prospect of being offered or of enjoying any useful or worthwhile occupation. They spent their time in a whirl of trivial social activities. They now went abroad for long periods of time. Wallis was restless and discontented and no doubt found Edward's dog-like devotion somewhat cloying. She formed a relationship with an American socialite millionaire which attracted the attention of the American press. Duff Cooper reported in June 1951 on their return from America: "She is causing a great deal of scandal here (France) as she did there (America).The Duke said he wanted

266 Norwich, p 403
267 Ibid p 412
268 Ibid p 467
269 Shawcross p 439

to have a word with me—I feared he might be going to discuss his domestic difficulties but all he wanted – was help with a speech."[270]

Between 1948 and 1950, Edward wrote his autobiography which was published in 1951 under the title of *A King's Story*, which dealt with his life until the abdication and was dedicated to Wallis. She visited London but, when King George VI died in 1952, Edward attended the funeral alone, as he did at Queen Mary's funeral in 1953. Neither were invited to Queen Elizabeth's Coronation in 1953. Edward seemed to divide his time between gardening, playing golf and a social round. As Ziegler wrote "It was not a crowded life but no less eventful than most men of more than sixty; it is only when it is compared with what might have been if the Duke had been more ambitious or dedicated that its triviality becomes so obvious."[271]

In 1958, Edward suffered a serious attack of shingles and he underwent a number of serious operations both in England and the United States. Wallis was in London and met the Queen for the first time while Edward was in hospital and they both attended the memorial service for the Princess Royal. In 1967, the Queen invited them both to the dedication of a plaque to Queen Mary outside Marlborough House. While Edward was invited to the investiture of Prince Charles as Prince of Wales and Wallis was not, he found an excuse not to go. By 1970, he had cancer of the throat and endured a long and painful illness and in May 1972, he died. His funeral was attended by all the Royal Family except the Duke of Gloucester who was ill and Wallis stayed with the Queen at Buckingham Palace. Thereafter she became increasingly frail and suffered from dementia. She suffered several falls and broke her hip twice. The rest of her life was spent as a recluse. She died in April 1986 and was buried next to Edward in the Royal Burial Ground in the gardens of Frogmore, near Windsor.

That Edward was deeply in love with Wallis is not in doubt. Giving up the throne of England, however little appetite he had

---

270 Ibid p 484
271 Ibid p 543

for it, is sufficient proof of his devotion. The public perception of Wallis at the time of the Abdication and for a good time afterwards was that of a rich ambitious American socialite on the make, who got her claws firmly into Edward and would not let go. She was not prepared to give him up and, even if she had wanted to, he was determined to stay with her. History may be a bit kinder to her now than that. Even if her love for him was driven by social climbing, there is no doubt that she provided him with a life as happy as it could have been in the circumstances. Not everyone now accepts that she made no effort to persuade him to renounce her rather than the throne. She was flattered by his position as Prince of Wales and he was flattered by her personality. "When Adam delved and Eve span, who was then the gentleman?"

CHAPTER EIGHTEEN

BOB BOOTHBY AND DOROTHY MACMILLAN

In 1929, Robert Boothby, MP was aged 29 and Dorothy Macmillan was much the same age. She was the third daughter of the Duke of Devonshire and was now married to Harold Macmillan, also a Conservative MP. They had first met at the Boothby family home, Beechwood, in Edinburgh in 1928 and had been on a golfing holiday at Gleneagles. In 1929, the Macmillans were invited to stay by Boothby's parents and to enjoy some shooting. There Boothby and Dorothy fell in love and started an affair. Who was the predator and who was the prey has been the subject of acute controversy since the matter became public. The partisans of each side blame the other for what happened. On the one side, Boothby is portrayed as a bounder who seduced a colleague's wife, while Dorothy is described as an oversexed, possessive girl, seeking adventure, bored with her husband and anxious to be rid of him.

Boothby was born in 1900 and was brought up as a child in Edinburgh. His father was Joint Secretary of the Scottish Provident and was a distinguished golfer, becoming Captain of the Royal and Ancient. Boothby himself was also a devoted golfer. At the age of four he was able to read and write. He had a beautiful voice and an acute musical ear and music was to play an important part in his life. At the age of 13 he went to Eton and from there, after the war, to Magdelen College, Oxford, where he read history. After coming down from Oxford, he went to the English Bar and joined the Chambers of Walter Monckton, later Lord Monckton.

However a General Election was due to take place in 1923 and Boothby found himself standing as a Conservative candidate for the Orkney and Shetland constituency. His good looks, youth, charm, fine speaking voice and intelligence impressed the electorate, but he was defeated by the Liberals who had held the seat for more than half a century. The East Aberdeenshire Unionist Association had been much impressed by his performance at Shetland and Orkney and invited Boothby to be their candidate. Boothby had also attracted the attention of the Conservative leader, Stanley Baldwin, who was now in opposition, having lost the general election. Baldwin invited Boothby to join his small staff. They subsequently became close friends. In October 1924 there was another general election and Boothby was elected with a majority of over 2,500. He was to be the member for East Aberdeenshire for over thirty years until in 1959, when he accepted a life peerage. He gave up the Bar when he became an MP and took up some journalism. Later, he was to become a partner in the City broking firm of Chase, Henderson and Tennant. In 1926, he became Churchill's Parliamentary Private Secretary. It was the beginning of a friendship which was to have many ups and downs and reached its lowest point over the affair of the Czech assets in 1941.

Harold Macmillan, who was to be the third party in the ménage a trois, which was now about to develop, had been born in 1894. His family, though descended from crofters in Scotland, owned and ran a most successful world-wide publishing business. The firm had been started by Macmillan's grandfather and great-uncle, who had bought a bookshop in Cambridge. They published their first book in 1843. In 1906, Macmillan secured the third scholarship to Eton but left early because of ill health. However, he was able to win a classical exhibition to Balliol College, Oxford where got a first class degree in Honour Mods. The onset of the First World War saw Macmillan join the Army. In the Battle of Loos in1915, serving in the Guards Division, he was wounded in the head and received a bullet through his right hand. In the battle of the Somme in 1916, he was badly wounded in the thigh and pelvis with the result that he was in hospital for over two years. In 1919, Macmillan was invited to be an ADC to the Duke of Devonshire, then Governor General of Canada. Macmillan's mother was a friend of the Duke's mother and arranged it. While there, he met Dorothy, then aged 19. They fell in love and, in April 1920, they were married. The marriage of Harold and Dorothy Macmillan is one of the most complex episodes in two notable complex lives – happy and tragic, by turns, before ending in a sunset era of the deepest devotion "calm of mind, all passions spent."[272]

Dorothy was born in 1900 and was privately educated at the various Cavendish houses. Her father became the Duke of Devonshire in 1908 and the family owned Chatsworth House and Hardwick Hall in Derbyshire, Bolton Abbey in Yorkshire, Compton Place in Eastbourne and Lismore Castle in Southern Ireland. The Devonshires could trace their ancestry to Bess of Hardwick, whose son became Earl of Devonshire in 1618. The dukedom was created in 1694.Some of the dukes were given to gambling and much infidelity. Some, like the eighth and ninth Duke, became politicians. The former, as the Marquis of Hartington had been in Lord Salisbury's Cabinet. The latter was Financial Secretary to the Treasury under Balfour, was Civil Lord of the Admiralty in Asquith's Coalition Government and subsequently served in the Cabinet, between1922-1924, as Colonial Secretary.

Dorothy was described as having an outdoor life which had little place for books and little interest in ideas. She was an earthy girl, keen on golfing and riding and bursting with bucolic health.[273] The Cavendish girls did not dress well. They had no need to show off their wealth. Dorothy was a good judge of character, was friendly and outgoing, devoid of snobbery and, while brought up in politics, was somewhat unworldly. The picture of Macmillan as Supermac is far removed from how he was regarded at this time.

---

272 Thorpe D.R. *Supermac. The Life of Harold Macmillan.* (Chatto and Windus, London 2010) p 67
273 Davenport-Hines, Richard. *The Macmillans.* (Mandarin Paperbacks. London 1993) pp 163-164

His Cavendish in-laws disliked him and were so bored by him that there was intense family competition not to sit next to him at meals. His teeth were malformed, his clothes were scruffy and poor, he had a moustache which was in sore need of attention, but above all he was rated by them and by others as the most stupendously boring man they had ever met. They could not understand why the vivacious and attractive Dorothy had ever married him.[274] There were two other problems in the marriage. His mother, Nellie, was overbearing and was a constant intruding shadow over them both. Macmillan, although completely infatuated with Dorothy, was unenthusiastic as a lover, while she was high spirited, warm and emotional, and craved excitement and drama.

After the marriage they lived at Chester Square and Birch Grove. In 1921, their son Maurice was born, followed by two daughters, Carol in 1923 and Catherine in 1926. Macmillan became a partner in the family publishing company. In 1923, he stood as the Conservative candidate at Stockton on Tees and came within seventy three votes of defeating the Liberal incumbent. In the next General Election, in 1924, he succeeded in winning the seat with a substantial majority. His contributions to debates in the House of Commons were limited and unimpressive but, in 1927, together with Boothby, Oliver Stanley and John Loder, he produced a booklet called *"Industry and the State."* It was an attempt to steer a path between outright capitalism and collectivism. Amongst the ideas were the need for larger scale manufacturing, for collective bargaining to be made statutory and for joint industrial councils to be given greater powers. It was strongly interventionist and very anti laisser-faire. The booklet was well received by some but was regarded by others as woolly socialism.

Macmillan was regarded as one of the new progressive members who banded together and were dubbed "the YMCA", by fellow members. They were dedicated to improving industrial

---

274 Rhodes James, Robert. *Bob Boothby*. (Hodder & Stoughton. London 1991) pp 112-113

relations and trying to ensure the rationalisation of uncompetitive British Industries. In particular Macmillan was much moved by the high rate of unemployment in Stockton. Boothby was also a member of this group and he and Macmillan cooperated closely. Boothby had been a strong supporter of Baldwin's desire for social unity and particularly of an understanding attitude towards the trade unions. One spin off from the booklet was to persuade Boothby's master, Churchill to re-rate industry in his Derating Bill in 1929. In the General Election in 1929, Boothby's majority increased, thanks to the absence of a Liberal candidate. Macmillan, however, as a result of Baldwin's election slogan "Safety First" was defeated by the Labour candidate. In 1929, Boothby's career after a successful period as Churchill's PPS and with a safe parliamentary seat, seemed set for the highest honours. Macmillan having lost his seat, and his wife to Boothby, was now faced with a double catastrophe which could only have (and did have) the effect of tearing him apart.

Boothby's description of himself was very accurate. He admired and envied Lloyd George's private life and his ability to get away with "two wives, two homes and two families."[275] He was a flamboyant character, full of fun and good humour, a fine speaker, the coming man, socially at ease wherever he went and dashingly handsome. The Cavendish women were reputed to be highly sexed and the contrast between the rather staid Macmillan and the romantic Boothby could not be more marked. Dorothy was a very determined woman. Boothby subsequently described her in this way: "She was always interested in power—she never suffered a pang of remorse—she was certainly not the sweet, simple, good quiet lady—Several times I got engaged, once in Venice, but Dorothy came all the way from Chatsworth to pursue me there—she was absolutely unafraid of anything—she broke off my engagement and stopped me twice more from getting married—she was relentless, there was a streak of cruelty in her—and very selfish."[276] He added on another occasion:

275 Boothby, Robert. *Recollections of a Rebel* (London 1978) p 160.
276 Horne, Alistair. *Macmillan 1891-1956* (Macmillan. London.1990) p 87

"What Dorothy wanted and needed was emotion on the scale of Isolde. This Harold could not give her and I could. She was on the whole one of the most selfish and possessive woman I have ever met."[277]

The menage a trois was conducted with far less publicity than would obtain today. Dorothy used to accompany both Boothby and Macmillan separately on holidays. Divorce was quite out of the question. For both men it would have been political suicide and so they continued together, until, in 1935, Boothby married Dorothy's cousin, Diana Cavendish. The marriage was not a success and ended after some two years. Despite his views of Dorothy's selfishness, they continued to see each other throughout the rest of her life, sometimes to visit and sometimes to go on holiday together. In 1967, a year after Dorothy's death, Boothby married again and was to have twenty years of happy married life. One of the victims of this relationship was Sarah, a daughter born to Dorothy in 1930. There is much speculation as to who her father was. It seems to have been accepted at the time that it was Boothby but he is alleged to have told Macmillan that he was not.[278] Dorothy thought she was Boothby's child. Whatever the truth, the impact of discovering, in her teens, that Macmillan might not be her father had a devastating effect on her life. She had an abortion, married unhappily, took to drink and died sadly in 1970.

The subsequent careers of Boothby and Macmillan followed very different paths. While, in 1929, Boothby recently returned as an MP and having been PPS to Churchill seemed on the brink of a meteoric political career. Macmillan, without a seat, and deprived of a wife, was at the nadir of his life. In the summer of 1931, he had something of a nervous breakdown. But fate has a way of playing tricks and, while Boothby's career was thereafter on a gradual downward slope, Macmillan's was, over several decades, to reach the highest level in politics. Macmillan stood again in the General Election in 1931 and with Liberal support, he

---

277 *Supermac.* p 98
278 Ibid p 100

regained his seat at Stockton with a majority of some 11,000. He and Boothby were now fellow MPs again though not in office and were regarded by the Conservative hierarchy with considerable suspicion for their views on industrial relations and their support for Churchill over appeasement.

For Boothby the affair of the Czech Assets in 1938, and the subsequent Select Committee report in 1940, was to have a devastating effect on his political career. He was forced to resign as a minister and although he was re –elected as an MP he would never again hold any sort of office. The Czech Assets Affair had its origin in Boothby's friendship with an Austrian called Richard Weininger. Weininger had gained and lost a fortune on the stock market before the First World War. In 1923, he became a Czech citizen, living in Munich and Berlin and having business interests in England and Czechoslovakia. In 1938, he left Berlin for Prague. Boothby had, by then, become interested in the future of Czechoslovakia, threatened as it was by Germany. As an MP, he had visited the country in June and September 1938. In January 1939, Weininger asked Boothby to help him unfreeze his wife's assets which were blocked by the Czech Banks as a result of the Munich Agreement. They agreed that Boothby would receive 10% of any assets that he recovered. The Bank of England and the Treasury gave instructions that the amount of claims by British holders of obligations (including the Weingingers) should be validated and paid by the Treasury.

At this time Boothby was in some financial difficulty and had obtained a temporary loan. He was anxious to secure the unfreezing of the assets and get his commission. He was elected Chairman of the Committee set up to secure payments for some of the claimants without disclosing his interest. He thereafter badgered the Treasury to settle the claims. Not all the claimants wanted to be represented by Boothby and Boothby put them under some pressure with the result that they complained. The Treasury believed that the Committee was involved in a business venture and demanded that it be wound up. It was. Boothby carried on negotiating with the Treasury and wrote a number of letters to the authorities, as did solicitors purporting to act on his behalf. When The Czechoslovakia (Financial Claims and Refugees) Bill was debated, Boothby remained silent about his financial interest in the Bill.

In October 1940, Churchill, now Prime Minister, sent for Boothby and told him that he was proposing to set up a Select Committee of the House of Commons to "investigate the conduct and activities of Mr Boothby in connection with the payment out of assets in this country—and in particular to consider whether the conduct of the Honourable Member was contrary to the usage or derogatory to the dignity of the House or inconsistent with the standards which Parliament is entitled to expect from its members." The Committee reported adversely to Boothby. They found that he had an expectation of benefit, which had never been disclosed and that his services to enable the Weiningers to get their money speedily, had been engaged on the basis that he would be paid commission on the result. The Committee found his conduct was—"inconsistent with the standards which Parliament is entitled to expect from its Members." Boothby resigned as Parliamentary Secretary to the Ministry of Food and retired to the back benches. When Churchill again became Prime Minister, in 1951, no post was offered to Boothby. In July 1958, Boothby wrote to Macmillan asking for a peerage. Macmillan offered a hereditary peerage. Boothby chose the latter and became Baron Boothby of Buchan and Rattray Head. He became Rector of St Andrews and something of a TV personality. He died in 1986.

Macmillan's career took an upward turn during the war. He became Under Secretary at the Ministry of Supply and then Under Secretary at the Colonial Office. But his next step was to put him at the forefront of politics. He became the British Minister Resident in North Africa with Cabinet rank. Here he was dealing not only with political problems in Africa and Italy, but also dealing at first hand with the Allied Commander, General Eisenhower and the top British and French Military Commanders. Subsequently he was in charge of the Control Commission in Greece. When Churchill became Prime Minister again, in 1951,

Macmillan was successively Housing Minister, Minister of Defence and, under Eden, Foreign Secretary and Chancellor of the Exchequer. When Eden resigned, Macmillan became Prime Minister. Although Dorothy continued to see Boothby as a loving friend, she became a devoted wife to Macmillan and proved to be a wonderful help and inspiration to him He also died in 1986

CHAPTER NINETEEN

MAUNDY GREGORY

The sale of honours by those in a position to award them (or their agents on their behalf) is a good example of the exercise of the power of the predator over the prey. In modern times, the most notorious was Maundy Gregory who sold honours on Lloyd George's behalf in the 1920s in order to provide Lloyd George with a personal fund. The prey were often undeserving characters who had made a great deal of money in the war and. who now wished to acquire the respectability which they believed attached to the award of an honour.

The reward of honours to loyal friends of the Crown or of a Government for their support, either by offering financial or military help, has a long history, going back several hundred years. Appointing peers to ensure a government majority in the House of Lords probably started in the early 17th century. The creation of press barons for supporting the policies of the government started in the late 19th century. As well as titles, many of those supporters were given vast tracts of land. The slaughter of the nobility in the Wars of the Roses, which ended with the Battle of Bosworth Field in 1485 and the accession of Henry VII, is thought to have resulted in the elevation of many new peers including the Russell family, who became Dukes of Bedford and the Cavendish family who became Dukes of Devonshire. It is not suggested that anything other than service was involved. Elizabeth, in her reign of nearly forty five years, only created eight peerages.

But things changed materially in the 17th Century with the Stuarts on the throne. They needed money and also to cope with Parliament. Between 1603 and 1609 some seventy peerages were created, most of which were purchased. The practice was continued under both Charles II and James II. It was done openly and was a private arrangement between King and subject. It was not only the sale of peerages which attracted the Kings as means of raising revenues. A lesser honour of a Baronetcy, hereditary in some cases, had first been introduced in Edward III's reign but had fallen into desuetude. In order to raise funds for settling the problems of Ulster, James I revived the Order in 1611 and made it hereditary. Initially there were not enough applicants and the price charged had to be reduced. There was to be no limitation on numbers and gradually they grew. At the same time, Dukedoms continued to be awarded by the Crown throughout the period up to about 1740.

Thereafter there was a change in the practice of awarding honours. Hitherto it had been the Crown who had been responsible and the purpose was essentially to raise money for their personal use. That was no longer necessary. It was now the responsibility of the Government, through Parliament, to raise the money needed by them and to ensure that the necessary legislation passed seamlessly through the House of Commons and the House of Lords. To that end. the Government (through the Prime Minister) needed to be able to control Parliament, a quite different object of selling honours from that of the Kings. In 1783, Pitt (the Prime Minister) managed not only to create sufficient Peers to have a permanent Tory majority in the House of Lords, but also to have control of the House of Commons by ensuring that patrons of boroughs, responsible for elections, were rewarded with honours. Until boroughs were abolished in 1832 the practice continued but direct payment for honours was now no longer an issue. Still there remained a criticism, which obtains today, that a financial contribution to a political party fund (which is an indirect payment) should not be a factor in considering an award of an honour. However election expenses continued to rise and political parties were often in debt, and for that reason, during the first part of the 20th Century, all governments continued to award honours to those who had made financial contribution to their Party Fund. It continues today. In addition Lloyd George gave Fleet Street newspaper proprietors a whole range of honours in the expectation of bribing them to give his Government support. In the years, between 1918 and 1922, the Press received some forty-nine Peerages, Privy Councillorships, Baronetcies and Knighthoods.[279]

From 1919, Lloyd George had serious problems over finances. It arose in this way. In 1916 he had become Prime Minister, in place of Asquith with a coalition Government. In 1918 there was the "Maurice" debate (about the adequacy of the provision, by Lloyd George, of munitions for the troops in France.) Some Liberals (mostly supporters of Asquith) voted against the Government. In the ensuing General Election, Lloyd George gave his support (known as a coupon] to those who had voted for him in the debate, thus excluding a large part of the Liberal party who came to be known as the Asquithian Liberals. However, the latter had their hands on the Liberal party funds which Lloyd George needed for his election expenses. It was therefore necessary for him to find a way to acquire what was essentially to be a private fund. To do this he engaged the Chief Whip, Freddy Guest and his press agent and political adviser, Sir William Sutherland. The latter had been prominent in helping Lloyd George over the "Maurice" debate. They, in turn, recruited Maundy Gregory (among others) who was to devise a whole new approach to the existing system of awarding honours.

Maundy Gregory was born on 1 July 1877, the son of a clergyman. He was educated at a local school and in 1895 went up to Oxford University as a non-collegiate student. He left without a degree. His father died shortly afterwards and Gregory found modest employment as an assistant master at a preparatory school for which post he was singularly ill-suited. Eventually he gave this up, became a drawing room entertainer and then went into the theatre, first as a manager and then as a professional actor. His first year in this role proved remarkably successful. But he decided that management was his forte. After a period of employment in this capacity, he decided to set up on his own and

---

279 Macmillan, Gerald. *Honours for Sale.* (The Richards Press. Charles Street. London 1954) pp 220-244

had a great success with his production of *Dorothy*. It was to be followed by a charity show in aid of the Lord Mayor's fund, with the Lord Mayor and Sheriffs due to attend. Failure to pay the salary of the musicians brought an end to the play and to Gregory's involvement with the stage.[280]

It is known that he joined the Household Battalion and then the Irish Guards during the War but saw no fighting. There is some suggestion that he was engaged in counter espionage work but like everything about Gregory, most of his life history which he described, was wildly exaggerated. From somewhere, he seems to have been able to acquire wealth and now presented a different persona, well dressed, bedecked with jewels, gold watches and similar ostentatious baubles including a fine diamond which had belonged to the Grand Duchess Anastasia. He managed to acquire a range of Orders from Foreign Royal families. He set himself up in well-furnished offices in Parliament Street in London, staffed by chosen messengers dressed to resemble Government messengers. To maintain a role of respectability, he acquired a large library and a collection of statuettes. He talked incessantly about distinguished people, with whom he claimed acquaintance, and often pretended to be talking on the phone to Buckingham Palace or Number 10 Downing Street to impress a visitor.

Another ploy to impress strangers with his importance was to engage a prominent guest in conversation at a public dinner and thereafter quote his views as if they were lifelong friends. By these methods, he gradually had an unrivalled collection of the "great and the good," including exiled Foreign Royalty, whose friendship he exploited outrageously. Entertaining in lavish style enabled him to increase his social standing yet further. But his most useful vehicle for furthering his ambitions was to publish, in August 1919, *The Whitehall Gazette and St James Review*, (known familiarly as "*The Whitehall Gazette*").

It was a brilliant public relations exercise because its appearance, indistinguishable from an official government publication like "*The London Gazette*", gave the impression that it was a high

---

280 Ibid pp 95-109

class document, of great weight and distinction, and also that it had royal patronage. Its circulation was almost entirely complimentary but by providing free copies to influential bodies such as clubs, embassies and politicians it had a readership out of all proportion to its production. One of the features of the paper was the constant reference to distinguished establishment figures with whom Gregory was able to claim a close relationship. By giving some of them the opportunity to publicise themselves in *"The Whitehall Gazette"* and charging them for the privilege, Gregory not only made money but widened his circle of influential figures. They included foreign dignitaries and celebrities. Thus it enabled him to meet a great many people only too anxious to pay substantial sums to be awarded some honour.

The other aspect of *"The Whitehall Gazette"* was that, from its design and content, it gave the impression that it enjoyed Official Patronage. This was achieved by its use of blue stiff paper similar to other Government publications, in its lay out and typography. A further device was the use of regular advertisements for the purchase of Savings Certificates, for contributions to King George's Fund for Sailors, for contributions to the Officers' Association and for the purchase of Treasury Bonds.[281] One other part of Gregory's publicity armoury was his acquisition of the Ambassador Club in 1926. It was an all-male luncheon club during the day and in the evening a night club for "the bright young things." It acquired a certain *louche* reputation. It attracted many distinguished and influential people and it became a favourite luncheon meeting place for MPs. Gregory installed a direct telephone line to the House of Commons for their benefit. A frequent visitor was the Prince of Wales and other visitors included King George and Prince Paul of Greece. It was a place to which the "great and the good" came and from which Gregory was able to glean a volume of information necessary for the project of advancing himself.[282]

---

281 Cullen, Tom. *Maundy Gregory* (The Bodley Head. London 1974) pp 99-101
282 Ibid. pp 121-122

Gregory's involvement in the Honours business is thought to have its origin in his contact with the Liberal Chief Whip, Lord Murray of Ellibank and his friend Captain Guest, subsequently Coalition Liberal Chief Whip. In the 1920s there were a number of touts operating in the honours brokerage business. It was Guest's responsibility to find someone to raise very substantial amounts for Lloyd George's private fund. Gregory fitted the criterion of being politically neutral, ostensibly a gentleman and having an occupation for which *"The Whitehall Gazette"* provided a suitable cover.[283] Other competitors were soon removed from contention.

The situation after the war was ripe for exploitation. There were some 340,000 wealthy candidates in England in 1919 who had made vast profits from the war and who now wanted the respectability which accompanied the award of a title.[284] The price for a knighthood was £10,000-12,000, for a baronetcy the going rate was £30,000-40,000, though John Stewart, (a whiskey distiller and a bootlegging friend of Lloyd George) paid £50,000, and for a peerage £50,000 was demanded. There were other honours for Gregory to sell. The recently introduced OBE was now an honour much sought after. In four years, some 25,000 were awarded. Gregory also managed to persuade a number of customers who were likely, legitimately, to receive an award, to pay for the privilege without their realising that they would have received the award in any event.

Some of the recommendations for honours were heavily criticised. Rowland Hodge was made a baronet. During the war he had been a food hoarder. Sir William Vestey was made a Baron. He was a wartime tax dodger. But it was the barony conferred on Sir Joseph Robinson in the 1922 Birthday Honours list which caused a public scandal and had political consequences. He had paid £30,000 instead of the £50,000 for which Gregory had originally asked. He had, as recently as November 1921, been convicted of fraud by purchasing the freehold of mining properties

---

283 Ibid pp 92-95
284 Ibid p 107

for himself and then selling them, at a grossly increased price, to the shareholders of his company. Because of the outcry, it was decided to withhold the honour and he was to be visited at his suite in the Savoy to be so informed. Being very deaf, he thought he was being asked for a larger contribution and got out his cheque book and asked "How much more?!"

Frances Stevenson wrote about honours: "I preferred not to be involved in the honours business. I found it very difficult to be polite to people who came to press their claims to recognition. There was one man who came regularly before each honours list to ask for a title—not for himself, he said, because he was not interested in titles but solely for the sake of his wife. Then his wife died, and I thought, well, we shall hear no more of this title. I was mistaken. Quite unashamed, the man turned up before the honours list, saying that his wife would have wished him to."[285] A number of similar cases had the effect of persuading the Conservative members of the Coalition that Lloyd George was not a man they could trust and they decided to come out of the Coalition. The Liberals were never again to be in sole office.

One of the last acts of Lloyd George, as Prime Minister, was to set up a Royal Commission on Honours. This was the result of Parliamentary pressure. On 17 July 1922, there was a full-scale debate in the House of Commons on the motion "that a Select Committee of seven members of this House be appointed to join with the Committee of the Lords to consider the present methods of submitting names of persons for honours—and to report what changes are desirable". Lloyd George grudgingly agreed to a Royal Commission but confined its terms of reference "to advise on the procedure to be adopted *in the future.*" (My emphasis.)[286] The Commission proposed that a Committee of three Privy Councillors should scrutiny the Prime Minister's list but also, more importantly, from Gregory's viewpoint, was the proposal for a short Act imposing penalties for receiving or making payments for honours.

285 Lloyd George, Frances. P 208
286 *H o C Debates. 5th Series vol 156 1922 col 1769*

In August 1925, the Honours (Prevention of Abuses) Act became law. This put some damper on his trafficking of honours but Gregory was able to make money by pretending to be able to procure honours and receiving money, knowing that the victim could not complain at not receiving the honour, because he too would be guilty of a criminal offence. Gregory also diversified activities by selling foreign titles and decorations. His appointment as a Commander of the Order of St John in June 1931, opened up a new network of customers for these honours, as did his elevation in the hierarchy of the Catholic Church in 1932. By September, he had received the Grand Cross of the Holy Sepulchre Order and was now the Patriarch's special representative in England. This position enabled him to sell papal honours without any legal sanction.[287] He needed the money because, in 1923, Sir George Watson had given Gregory £30,000 in bonds, almost certainly for some honour. Time passed and when Sir George died in 1930, there had been no honour. The executors sued and, in 1932, Gregory was forced to settle by paying £10,000 at once, and the balance over the next two years.[288] Although his friend Mrs Rosse, who had died in very suspicious circumstances, had made a will leaving Gregory as the sole beneficiary of her estate of £18,000, it was not enough to ward off the financial crisis which he now faced.

It was this financial crisis which was the cause of Gregory's disastrous decision to approach Lt Commander Leake. R.N. with the offer of a knighthood. That resulted in Gregory's appearance at Bow Street Magistrate's Court on 16 February 1933, charged with an offence under the Act, in trying to obtain £10,000 from Leake as an inducement for procuring a knighthood. Leake had been a war hero, having won a DSO in the blockade of the Zeebrugge Canal, led by Admiral of the Fleet, Sir Roger Keyes, in April 1918. Gregory had used Douglas Moffat as his agent to solicit enquiries for honours. After a letter and telephone call to Leake, Moffat met him and showed him a copy of "*The Whitehall*

---

287 Cullen p 169
288 Ibid p 164

Gazette" containing a report of a dinner at the Ambassador Club. Moffatt indicated that Gregory, named prominently in the report, could get him a knighthood. It was arranged that he should meet Gregory. At their meeting, Gregory indicated a knighthood could be obtained on payment of £10.000. After several meetings, during which Leake asked for time to consider, he finally told Gregory that he did not wish to continue. Leake had already reported the matter to the authorities. Gregory pleaded guilty to the single offence charged and was sentenced to two months imprisonment in the second division and a fine of fifty pounds. After his release and now bankrupt, he left for France. At his creditors meeting, the executors of a shipowner with an estate of £600,000 claimed a sum of £13,000 as a loan. It was clearly money paid for an honour which was not received. There were other substantial claims relating to honours trafficking.[289] Gregory continued to live in France in some style until he died in Paris in 1941.The predator had had a long and successful innings, but, in the end, it was one of the prey who brought him down.

---

289 Macmillan pp 193-197

CHAPTER TWENTY

JOHN PROFUMO AND CHRISTINE KEELER

In 1961, John Profumo was Secretary of State for War in Harold Macmillan's Conservative Government. He was aged 46 and was married to the actress, Valerie Hobson. Christine Keeler was a call girl. At this time she was aged 19. In July 1961, they met at a house party at Cliveden owned by Lord Astor. They started an affair which lasted a few weeks. Because she was also having an affair with Yevgeni Ivanov, the assistant naval attaché at the Soviet Embassy, there was anxiety that there was a national security element in Profumo's relationship with Christine. The affair became a national scandal. It was known as "The Profumo Affair." In June 1963, he confessed that he had had relations with Christine and that he had told lies to the House of Commons, when in March, he had denied any sort of impropriety. Profumo resigned. Christine was subsequently prosecuted for an unrelated offence of perjury and served a prison sentence of nine months. There was a wave of sexual allegations, hotly pursued by a press to the delight of a prurient public. In the end it was left to Lord Denning's Report to bring some degree of balance to a story which had run wildly out of control.

Profumo was born on 30 January 1915, in London. His father was the 4th Baron Profumo, a barrister and diplomat of Italian origin, but Profumo never used the title. He was educated at Harrow and at Brasenose College, Oxford where he read law. During the war, he served in North Africa, Italy and France. He was mentioned in despatches and was awarded the OBE for gallant and distinguished service while serving on the staff of

Field Marshall Lord Alexander in Italy. He subsequently served as chief of staff to the British Mission to Japan. He was also awarded the Bronze Star Medal by the Americans. He ended the war as a Brigadier and left the Army in 1950.

His political career started at the age of 25. In 1940, while in the Army, he won a by election as a Conservative at Kettering, Northamptonshire. He lost his seat at the General Election in 1945 but in the 1950 General Election he won the safe seat at Stratford on Avon. When, in 1952, the Conservatives were returned to power, Profumo rapidly achieved a succession of important offices. He was Parliamentary Secretary to the Ministry of Civil Aviation in November 1952, Joint Parliamentary Secretary to the Ministry of Transport and Civil Aviation in November 1953, Parliamentary Undersecretary of State for the Colonies in January 1957 and, at the Foreign Office, in November 1958. Shortly thereafter he was promoted to be Minister of State for Foreign Affairs and, in July 1960, was Secretary of State for War. In 1954 he married the well known actress, Valerie Hobson.

Christine Keeler was born on 22 February 1942. Her father deserted her mother who later lived with Edward Huish in a converted railway carriage. Christine had no academic qualifications and her first job was a typing job. Other jobs followed. In April 1959, she gave birth to a son who died six days later. After working as a waitress in a restaurant, she was introduced to Peter Murray, who owned Murray's Cabaret Club in Soho. She was hired as a topless showgirl. Soon afterwards, she met Stephen Ward a well known society osteopath and went to live with him in Bayswater. She once described their relationship as that of brother and sister and that "there were never to be any sexual goings on between us". Ward was a portrait painter who included Prince Philip among his clients. He had a wide network of society friends and he introduced Christine to many of them. Keeler got to know Mandy Rice Davis who was to play a leading part in the Profumo affair and Maria Novotny who ran sex parties in London attended by the "great and the good". One such party, in December 1961, was to figure prominently in the subsequent scandal and involved naked men and women clad only in wisps of clothing. There was one particular man in just a mask and a tiny apron. His identity was to give rise to much speculation and rumour which was investigated by Lord Denning who was appointed to conduct an Inquiry into the security aspects of the affair.[290]

Ward was a friend of Lord Astor and had the use of a cottage on the estate at Cliveden. Another friend was Kevin Wagstaffe of MI5. He asked Ward to keep an eye on Ivanov, the assistant Russian Naval attache. Ward had met him at lunch in January 1961 and agreed to do so. Despite the anxieties by the security services about the close relationships between Christine, Ivanov, Profumo and Ward, Denning wrote: "in no case have I found any evidence for believing that national security has been or may be endangered."[291] In July 1961, Profumo was staying with his wife at Cliveden. Also there were Christine, Ward, and others. Profumo met Christine and, shortly thereafter, they began an affair. Meanwhile unknown to Profumo, Christine was also having sex with Ivanov and with a West Indian drug dealer, Johnny Edgecombe. MI5 were naturally concerned about Profumo's relation with Christine and the Cabinet Secretary warned Profumo about it. On 9 August 1961, Profumo wrote a letter to Christine, breaking off the affair. This became known as the "Darling" letter. It read "Darling, In great haste and because I can get no reply from your phone—Alas something's blown up tomorrow night and I can't therefore make it. I'm terribly sorry especially as I leave the nest day for various trips and then a holiday so won't be able to see you again until sometime in September. Blast it. Please take great care of yourself and don't run away. Love J." The association finished in December 1961. In January 1963, Christine sold the letter to the Sunday Pictorial.

So far the matter had remained unknown to the British public. Christine had also had an affair with another West Indian, Lucky Gordon. He and Edgecombe were rivals. In October, 1962, Edgecombe had slashed Gordon's face with a knife and, in

---

290 Lord Denning's Report Cmnd 2152(HMSO. London 1963) pp1-114
291 Ibid para 298

167

December, after Christine had refused to find a lawyer for Edgcombe, he turned up at Wimpole Street where Christine and Mandy were. When Christine refused to let him in, he started shooting. Subsequently she disappeared. The Police were now involved and rumours of Profumo's affair began to circulate. On 21 March 1963, during a debate in the House of Commons, three Labour MPs under cover of Parliamentary privilege raised questions with the Home Secretary about the relationship between Profumo and Christine and about her disappearance. She had left the country rather suddenly. George Wigg MP said "I ask—the Home Secretary to go to the despatch Box—he knows that the rumour to which I refer relates to Miss Christine Keeler and Miss Davies and a shooting by a West Indian—and on behalf of the Government categorically deny the truth of these rumours." Wigg was sure of his information, because, in early 1963, Christine had confided in John Lewis, a former MP, that she was concerned about being called as a witness to the shooting. During that conversation and subsequently, she told Lewis of her affair with Profumo, details of which Lewis retailed on a regular basis to his friend, Wigg.

Richard Crossman MP said: "By this evening a Paris newspaper may have published in full the rumours which have run round this House and the country and are touched upon day by day in the Press." Barbara Castle MP said: "It would suit the book of many people, no doubt, to deplore the avidity with which the press is at this moment pursuing the question of where Miss Christine Keeler has gone, the missing" call girl "and the vanished witness"—Mr Paget said "it is just a case of a minister having been found with a pretty girl and good luck to him but what if there is something else of much greater importance? What if it is a question of the perversion of justice which is at stake?"

On 22 March, Profumo made a statement in the House in which he said: "I understand that my name has been connected with the rumours about the disappearance of Miss Keeler— I last saw Miss Keeler in December 1961 and I have not seen her since. I have no idea where she is now. Any suggestion that I was in any way connected with or responsible for her absence from the trial at the Old Bailey is wholly and completely untrue. My wife and I first met Miss Keeler at a house party in July 1961, at Cliveden. Among a number of people there were Dr Stephen Ward, whom we already knew slightly, and a Mr Ivanov who was an attaché at the Soviet Embassy. My wife and I had a standing invitation to visit Dr Ward. Between July and December 1961, I met Miss Keeler on about half a dozen occasions at Dr Ward's flat, when I called in to see him and his friends. Miss Keeler and I were on friendly terms. There was no impropriety whatsoever in my acquaintanceship with Miss Keeler." He then threatened that any repetition of the rumours, unprotected by Parliamentary privilege, would result in litigation.[292]

In March, the French Newspaper, "*Paris Match*" published an article suggesting that Profumo had helped Keeler to disappear. He sued for libel in the French Courts and received a retraction and an apology. When in April, "*Tempo Illustrato*" published another story about Profumo and Christine, Profumo sued the publishers in this country and accepted an apology and a token sum for the libel, which he gave to an Army charity. Wigg did not give up. On 7 May, he raised the matter again under the pretence that national security was involved. He said: " I have in mind the case of Commander Ivanov, the Soviet Assistant Naval Attache, who came to this country and assiduously cultivated certain classes of the more diseased sections of our society—It must be obvious to everyone that stories of this kind spread far beyond this country—It is therefore in terms of the honour of this country as well as the security of Ministers—that rumours and stories of this sort should be dealt with, with alacrity—we must realise that we are dealing with a long term, grim battle which involves not only the security of this country, but the whole concept of the Western way of life."[293]

Wigg was motivated by a particular hatred of Profumo as a result of an earlier exchange in the House of Commons in which Wigg had been humiliated. In November 1962, he complained at

---

292 Ibid col 810
293 Ibid vol 677. cols 312-313

very great length about the deplorable conditions to which British troops in Kuwait had been exposed. Profumo, then War Minister, referred to letters from two Commanding officers which showed that Wigg's allegations were wildly exaggerated. Profumo said: "Perhaps, he (Wigg) will take what I now say in the spirit in which I now say it. I am sure that he has read a very wise and witty book by that great sportsman, Jack Leach, with the arresting title "*Sods I have cut on the Turf.*" In that book the author coins a new phrase. He refers to a stalking horse, which is apparently an animal which is frequently taken on to the course with the certainty of his winning, but which never quite wins. Afterwards, there is always a great deal of talk about its performance The Hon Member for Dudley (Wigg) formed his own views of the Kuwait operation in the very early days and when it did not turn out in the way he expected, he became his own stalking horse. It ran for about 1 1/2 hours this morning and was very good value for its money.—from the very beginning, he started with the idea of the Kuwait operations failing. He was sure it could not work."[294]

On 5 June, Profumo wrote a letter to the Prime Minister in which he admitted lying to the House. It read: "—I made a personal statement. At that time rumour had charged me with assisting in the disappearance of a witness and with being involved in some probable breach of security. So serious were these allegations that I allowed myself to think that my personal association, with that witness which had also been the subject of rumour, was by comparison, of minor importance only. I said that there had been no impropriety in this association. To my very deep regret I have to admit that this was not true, and that I misled you and my colleagues, and the House. I ask you to understand that I did this to protect, as I thought, my wife and family, who were equally misled as were my professional advisers. I have come to realise that by this deception. I have been guilty of a grave misdemeanour and despite the fact that there is no truth whatever in the other charges, I cannot remain a member of your administration, or of the House of Commons"

---

294 Ibid cols 1671-1672

The papers were now able to publish at will and the summer was replete with ever more scandalous stories. Lord Denning was invited by Macmillan to conduct an Enquiry into the security aspects of the Profumo Affair. He produced a report which rapidly became a best seller. In March, Edgecombe was sentenced to seven years imprisonment for a firearms offence. The police now brought proceedings against Ward for living off the immoral earnings of Mandy and Christine. After a few days of the trial, Ward who was on bail, committed suicide but was convicted in his absence. The general view is that whatever else he had done, he was wrongly convicted of those offences. The police had brought immense pressure on a number of witnesses. A good deal of the evidence was almost certainly false and the judge undoubtedly took a biased view against Ward. The evidence gave rise to a famous comment by Mandy. When prosecuting counsel suggested to her that Lord Astor had denied ever having met her or that he had had an affair with her, Mandy replied: "Well, he would, wouldn't he?"

The fallout from the affair was primarily political though it had its effect on the various individuals involved. On investigation, the idea that there was some security aspect to the events had no foundation. While rumours abounded and allegations flourished, there was simply no substance to any of them. Ivanov was sent back to Russia. He took no secrets with him. Ward and Profumo were not betraying State secrets and if Christine was seeking confidential information from Profumo, she certainly never received any. Profumo resigned from the Government, Parliament and the Privy Council. He went to work at Toynbee Hall, a Charity in the East End of London, doing menial tasks but eventually he became their chief fund raiser at which he was very successful. In 1975, he was awarded the CBE and at Margaret Thatcher's 70th birthday in 1995, he was seated next to the Queen. On 9 March 2006, after a massive heart attack he died.

Christine found various jobs under an assumed name, wrote a number of memoirs, was married twice and divorced and had two sons. Mandy went to Israel, took part in a number of film and TV productions, started some restaurants and nightclubs and made a series of pop records. She too wrote her memoirs. But it was on the political scene that there was the greatest impact. A sex scandal involving an important member of Macmillan's government, and the suggestion that the whole affair had been badly mishandled, led to a feeling that the Government was out of touch and had become something of a laughing stock. Cries for his resignation fell on deaf ears, but there is no doubt that the government was fatally wounded When, in September, Macmillan became ill, he was succeeded by Alec Douglas Home but, at the subsequent General Election in 1964, the Labour Party, under Harold Wilson, was swept back to power. Macmillan never came back and retired to the House of Lords.

CHAPTER TWENTY ONE

BELCHER AND HAMILTON

It is not always the case that a politician in a position of power is the predator. Sometimes, simply because he is in a position of power, he is the object of attention by someone wanting to use that power for his own benefit. The effect of that attention has in some cases proved disastrous. Two such members of Parliament were John Belcher and Neil Hamilton, who corruptly used their power for the benefit of third parties, and also for their own. They had the misfortune to suffer for their misdemeanours in the most public way.

Belcher was born in 1905. He went to an elementary school in Hammersmith and then gained a scholarship to Latymer Upper School. After a short period working for an estate agent, he became a railway clerk and then an official of the Railway Clerks Association. He was appointed as a delegate to the TUC and Labour Party. He married in 1927 and had three children. During the War, because of chronic intestinal disorders, he was unfit for military service and worked as a lecturer for the Ministry of Information. In the 1945 election, he became Labour MP for Sowerby in Yorkshire and, in 1946, he was to be appointed by Sir Stafford Cripps, President of the Board of Trade, to be Parliamentary Secretary to that Ministry. His job was to attend functions, trade shows, fairs and exhibitions, and to appear at social occasions such as dinners, lunches and cocktail parties. As he told the Tribunal, investigating his subsequent conduct, he regarded it as his job, in dealing with businessmen suspicious of a Labour Government, "to do all in my power to investigate not only the complaints but whether difficulties were being experienced."[295]

He wanted to disarm the natural suspicion of the business community because, if the Government wished to escape from the economic agony through which they were going, it had to engage with business and secure its trust. It was a period of extreme austerity when raw materials were in short supply and in great demand. Almost every business venture required government sanction and was subject to regulations, designed to protect the economy, which was in a parlous state. Rationing of food and petrol still continued long after the war and drink was in short supply. A thriving black market flourished in almost every commodity. Because Belcher was anxious to help businessmen and they were anxious to bend the ear of the minister by offering generous hospitality, there was always going to be a temptation and opportunity for any minister, who offered assistance, to be corrupted.

Belcher first met Sidney Stanley, (who was to bring about his downfall), in April 1947 at a dinner at the Garrick Hotel in Leicester Square. Stanley was of Polish origin, an undischarged bankrupt and with a 1933 deportation order outstanding against him. After their first meeting, Stanley became a friend of Belcher and a frequent visitor to the Board of Trade. He impressed Belcher with his apparent contacts in the business and financial world. He spent some £60,000 a year on entertaining to prove his point. Stanley offered to put up the Belcher family in a hotel at Margate and Bournemouth. Thereafter their friendship became more intimate. Belcher used to drop in to Stanley's flat in Park Lane and have a drink with him. Stanley bombarded Belcher with gifts of food and drink, and on one occasion gave him a new suit and a gold watch worth £60. There was lavish entertainment at boxing matches at Bethnal Green and the dog track at Harringay. For Belcher's birthday, Stanley gave an expensive dinner party for six at the Garter Club.

But it was in relation to the affairs of Harry Sherman that Belcher found himself in difficulties. Sherman was a football pool's promoter. The business necessarily required large quantities

295 Report of the Lynskey Tribunal 1949 Cmd 7617

of paper which were in very short supply. Their allocation was regulated by the Board of Trade. In 1948, Sherman and Stanley met at his flat. Stanley boasted of his friendship with Belcher and that he could fix up for Sherman to meet Belcher to discuss the allocation. Sherman and Stanley entered into some financial transactions as part of Stanley's reward for obtaining Belcher's help for Sherman. There was a real problem. Sherman had previously managed to avoid the relevant regulations and was to be the subject of a prosecution. Before it could be proceeded with, it was withdrawn. The Tribunal found that: "they were satisfied that Belcher's action in withdrawing the Sherman prosecution was influenced by the persuasion of Stanley, acting on Sherman's behalf, and that, because of the benefactions of Stanley to him, Belcher allowed himself to be improperly influenced".[296] The Tribunal also took into account that Belcher had delayed reporting allegations by Sherman to any higher authority and, in a letter to the Lord Chancellor, Belcher had not exhibited proper candour. Belcher had made himself accessible to Stanley, and his business associates.

Further, he had, on Stanley's behalf, intervened about the possibility of importing steel from the United States and, on another occasion, supported an application for the licence of a seaside hotel. The influence which Stanley exercised over Belcher was due to the sense of material obligation which Belcher had incurred. Other instances were less serious. A Glasgow distiller, Sir Michael Bloch, needed a licence for the import of sherry casks for his business. He found that the gift of fifty seven bottles of sherry, whiskey and burgundy, (almost unobtainable at this time in London.) supplied over two months, secured the necessary licence from Belcher. The Tribunal found that Belcher accepted the gifts "knowing the object with which they were made".[297] That Belcher "the prey" was influenced by Stanley "the predator," rather than the other way round, did not enable the Tribunal to exonerate Belcher from all responsibilities. Belcher resigned as an MP and

---

296 Ibid
297 Ibid

returned to his former job as a railway clerk. He retired in 1963 and died a year later.

Neil Hamilton was born on 9 March 1949 in Wales where he grew up. He joined the Conservative party at the age of 15. After he left the local grammar school he went to the University College of Wales. He was active in the Federation of Conservative students. Thereafter he went to Corpus College, Cambridge where he obtained a postgraduate law degree. After a period as a school teacher, during which he read for the Bar exams, he was called to the Bar and specialised in taxation. He gave up after about eight years. In 1974 he had stood unsuccessfully as a Conservative candidate at the General Election and he was again unsuccessful in 1979. However, in 1983, he was elected at Tatton. Hamilton was no stranger to controversy. He was on the right wing of politics and belonged to a variety of right-wing pressure groups. He joined a lobbying group, Ian Greer Associates, and was reprimanded by a Commons Selection Committee for failing to disclose that he was being paid to influence ministers. On another occasion, he was criticised for not declaring that he was being paid a fee for consultancy work on behalf of Strategy Network International, lobbying against anti-apartheid groups.

In 1984, Hamilton was the subject of a programme on *"Panorama"* which was critical of his right-wing views. The programme claimed that he had given a Nazi salute in Berlin. The BBC decided to settle the case of libel which Hamilton brought, citing the intimidation of witnesses they had wished to call. However, Phil Pedley, who was the former chairman of the Young Conservatives, and who had taken part in the Panorama programme and was also a defendant, refused to be party to the settlement and determined to fight on. A political row then blew up with the Labour party accusing the Conservatives of a cover up, in relation to witnesses. In the result, Hamilton, withdrew his case against Pedley and was ordered to pay Pedley's costs. In 1990, Margaret Thatcher appointed him a whip and subsequently John Major made him Minister for "deregulation and corporate affairs." 1994 was to see the start of litigation which was to prove disastrous for Hamilton, giving rise to "The Cash for Questions Enquiry." *The Guardian* published an article alleging that Hamilton and Tim Smith, another MP, had received cash in brown envelopes from Al-Fayed, the owner of Harrods, in order to ask questions in the House of Commons on behalf of Al-Fayed. Al-Fayed had been involved in a bitter battle with Lonhro for control of Harrods. The Department of Trade and Industry carried out an enquiry which was very critical of Al-Fayed. They declined to rescind the Report. He had tried twice to become a British citizen, both unsuccessfully. Eventually, it was announced that Al-Fayed would not be given an English passport.

Al-Fayed was not a person to take these setbacks lightly. Ian Greer, the lobbyist, went to see Al-Fayed and offered to help. He told Al-Fayed that a fee of £50,000 was required because he would have to pay Hamilton and Smith to ask questions on behalf of Al –Fayed. £ 2000 per question was agreed. Greer boasted that "You can hire M.Ps just like you rent a London Taxi." When *The Guardian* published an article critical of Hamilton, he and Greer sued for libel. In September 1996, they withdrew their actions. Smith admitted his guilt and resigned his ministerial post immediately. Hamilton decided to pursue a further action against *The Guardian*. However just before the start of the trial, Hamilton withdrew and paid *The Guardian's* legal costs. An enquiry by Sir George Downey, the Parliamentary Commissioner for Standards, found Hamilton had received some benefits for asking questions but on an appeal to a Parliamentary Committee, Downey's conclusions were not fully accepted.

However, Al-Fayed reported that Hamilton had asked for and received cash of over £100,000 together with Harrods' gift vouchers and a free holiday at the Ritz in Paris which Al-Fayed owned. Hamilton sued Al Fayed for libel denying that he had received anything from Al-Fayed. An attempt by Al-Fayed to strike out Hamilton's claim as an abuse of process was rejected by the Courts.[298] In November 1999, the libel action was heard before a judge and jury, who found unanimously in favour of

---

298 1999 1Weekly Law Reports pp 1569 - 1591

Al-Fayed. Because of the publicity about the allegations, Hamilton lost his seat at Tatton in the General Election. He had had a majority in 1992 of some 16,000. Now his opponent, Martin Bell, had a majority of some 11.000. In1991, Hamilton declared himself bankrupt. His subsequent political career was less dramatic. In 2011, he joined UKIP and became a member of the National Committee and Deputy Chairman. His attempt to become a member of the Wandsworth Borough Council ended in failure but, in 2016, he became a member of the Welsh Assembly.

Al–Fayed was born in Alexandra, Egypt in January 1929. His father was a schoolmaster. His background and rise in the business world, where he is said to be worth millions of pounds, is shrouded in mystery. It appears that for a short while he worked for his brother in law, Adnan Khashoggi, who was a well-known Saudi Arabian arms dealer. Thereafter he was involved in a shipping company before coming to England in the mid-1960s. He was involved in a number of financial businesses in Dubai and Brunei. Between 1975 and 1979 he was on the Board of Lonhro, the mining conglomerate, of which "Tiny" Rowland was the head.

But it was not until 1984, when he bought a 30% stake from Rowland in the House of Fraser, the then owners of Harrods, that Al-Fayed became a household name. In 1985, after one of the bitterest takeover battles in London, he bought the remaining House of Fraser shares. Rowland cried foul and persuaded the Government to set up an inquiry, which it did. It was highly critical of Al-Fayed and may have been one of the reasons for his failure to be granted citizenship. His son became involved with Princess Diana and was killed in the car crash in Paris with her. Al-Fayed's complaints at the inquiry that there was some form of conspiracy was rejected by the judge who conducted it. Al-Fayed left the country disillusioned and his reputation much diminished.

Al-Fayed and Stanley both thought that money could buy them what they most needed, which was influence in their personal and business arrangements, as well as prestige from their association with political figures. Belcher and Hamilton were greedy adventurers, prepared to be bribed for the opportunity to make a dishonest profit from what they knew was an amoral arrangement. They were the sufferers as well as Stanley and Al-Fayed, which might suggest that the former were the prey and not the predators. In one sense they were, because it was they, rather than Stanley or Al-Fayed, who offered their services for hire. But those in a positon of power, who can provide access to the fringes of government, are also acting as predators and they received their just deserts. All of them richly deserved each other.

CHAPTER TWENTY TWO

FIDEL CASTRO

Castro had a wife and a large number of one night stands. However, there were three women who were to play a particularly important part in the revolution which led to Castro's overthrow of the Batista regime in Cuba. They were Celia Sanchez, Teresa Casusos and Naty Revuelta. They were an extraordinary contingent of beautiful or intelligent women who, in effect, dedicated their lives to him and his cause. Without them, he might well not have succeeded. It is generally accepted that Fidel Castro was born on 13 August 1926. He was the illegitimate son of a successful Creole sugar plantation owner. At school he was a rebellious pupil, though he excelled at games. At 18, he went to a school in Havana run by Jesuit priests. His report read: "He has always distinguished himself in all courses relating to letters. Excellent in religion. He has been a true athlete—He will dedicate himself to a career in law and we have no doubt that, he will fill with brilliant pages, the book of his life".[299]

When he went to the University of Havana, his sporting prowess counted for nothing and he turned to politics. He joined the International Revolutionary Union (UIR) and gained a reputation as something of a hoodlum. In July 1947, he joined an expedition to invade Santo Domingo and overthrow the dictator, Tujillo. Government forces intercepted the expedition and Castro jumped overboard to avoid arrest. He was then involved in a riot in Bogota, where he had gone to demonstrate against an International

---

299 Quirk, Robert.E. *Fidel Castro* (W.W.Norton & Company. New York 1993)
    p 19

Conference of American States. He returned to University where he acquired a reputation as a campus gangster, being twice accused of murder. In October 1948 he married Mirta Díaz Balart, a student from a wealthy family through whom he was exposed to the lifestyle of the Cuban elite and whose father was linked to Batista, a former President of Cuba. In 1950, after five years at University, Castro was awarded a law degree. His practice as a lawyer was unsuccessful. In 1952 Batista executed a coup and again became President. Castro now turned his attention to national politics.

By 1953, he was beginning to organise an insurgent group opposed to Batsista, but, without weapons, they were powerless. This gave rise to the attack on 26 July 1953 on the Moncada Barracks, after which episode the "July 26 movement" was named. It was an inept affair. The barracks had not been reconnoitred. The insurgents got lost. They had insufficient fire power to attack a well-armed barracks and they retreated in considerable disarray, losing half their force, who were killed or captured. Castro himself was captured and in September was put on trial. He was sentenced to fifteen years imprisonment. His book *History will absolve me*, published later and said to contain his speech at trial, ensured that he obtained great publicity and prestige. After two years he was set free and went to live in Mexico. Here he continued to plot against the Batista regime.

Subsequently, he returned to Cuba with a small band of supporters in the yacht *Granma* and, with a guerrilla band, set up bases in the mountains. A number of women who became his mistresses, helped him with supplies and acted as couriers. Castro gradually built up his Army and, with increasing success, left the countryside and attacked cities. The US Government, which had supported the Batista regime, now started to lose confidence in him. It forced Batista to hold elections which, because of a massive boycott, was something of a disaster for Batista. He fled Cuba. Senior army generals, left in charge, sought to set up a military government. A call by Castro for a general strike was successful. The military were defeated and, in January 1959, Castro marched into Havana and became Cuba's new Prime Minister.

In 1957, Celia Sanchez had joined Castro. She was not the only woman in his life. Mostly they were one night stands, but she was the most faithful, and together with Teresa Casuso, looked after him like doting wives. For a month, he was engaged to Carmen Custudio. They had met when Castro was imprisoned in Mexico in 1956. While there, Teresa, a Cuban lady living in Mexico, went to visit Castro, accompanied by Carmen, who was her house guest. Carmen was a beautiful teenager and, when Castro first saw her, he was smitten. Teresa left her card with Castro and, when he was released from prison, he called at her house. Here he made himself at home but at the same time, pursuing Carmen, with whom he had fallen in love. He showered her with lavish presents. Now he smartened himself up, sought her parents' permission to marry and proposed. Carmen, however, was not prepared to be the wife of an adventurer in Cuba and decided to marry her former fiancé. That was the end of the romance with Carmen.

Celia and Teresa however were to remain constant companions to Castro. In 1956, in Mexico City, Castro was organising a guerrilla expedition to Cuba. He moved his guns into Teresa's house and then moved in himself. When Castro was broke, she lent him $50,000 to finance the purchase of a boat for the Cuban expedition. Her premises were raided by the Mexican police and when Castro's ammunition was found, Teresa ended up in prison. After she was released, she remained in Mexico, but, when the Batista regime collapsed, she was instrumental in taking charge of the Cuban Embassy in Mexico City. She was a dark, dashing, sophisticated, divorcee, older than Castro She had been involved in cinema productions and writing film scripts, novels and plays. She also served as a cultural attaché at the Cuban embassy. In January 1959, Teresa flew from Mexico to join Castro in Cuba, where he put her in charge of his appointments. Unsurprisingly, there was friction with Celia. When, in April 1959, he flew to the United States to meet the press, politicians and the Vice-President, he left Celia behind, but took Teresa. At the Cuban Embassy, where Castro hosted a reception, Teresa was by his side, glamorously dressed and made up like a First Lady.

Celia was born in 1920 and died in 1980. She joined the revolutionary movement in 1952, after the coup by Batista. Her part was to act as courier carrying secrets and banknotes to finance the uprising. She was one of the founders of the July 26th movement. She helped to organise volunteers to arrange for the landing of Castro and his followers in Cuba, and thereafter to secure reinforcements. She was wanted by the Batista police and when it was unsafe for her to stay on the plains, she went to join Castro in the Sierra Maestra. According to one view: "she was more a mother-cum-secretary to him than a surrogate wife. Several years older than him, she lavished maternal attention on him—she fussed over him, praised him, picked up his cigar butts, cleaned his boots, arranged his meals and his business affairs and wrote out most of his letters.—She was clearly in charge of the camp and gave orders to the men—ultimately she was powerful in her own right."[300] She was present at a number of the important rebel attacks. In November 1957, she took part in the battle of Guisa. She was at the forefront of the struggle in the Sierra Maestra, where the revolution started, and then into the Oriente province where the attack on the Estrada Palma sugar factory took place.

In 1957, she was described "as an essential pillar of the revolutionary movement. Castro relied increasingly on her to arrange for supplies and ammunition for his rebel army. "If he wanted to share his enthusiasms and his ambitions, he wrote to Celia. Soon she moved permanently to the Sierra Maestra. Probably she shared his bed as well."[301] When, in January 1959, Batista resigned, and Castro was left with huge problems of organisation of the economic and political system of the country, he was able to leave the Sierra Maestra in Celia's capable hands. She used large sums of money obtained from landowners and businessmen to pay bills run up by rebel forces without reference to Castro. Teresa was always regarded as a rival and sometimes Castro chose one to accompany him on a visit and left the other behind. Early in 1960, he was at a dinner with Teresa, which Celia

---

300 Quirk. p 154
301 Ibid

declined to attend, but Celia was invited without Teresa to a ceremony at Turquino Peak, the site of one of Castro's early victories. In March 1962, when the government announced the formation of a party secretariat, Castro became first Secretary and his brother, Raul, second Secretary. Celia was appointed to be Secretary to the Presidency of the Council of Ministers with a seat in the Cabinet. She served in the Department of Services of the Council of State, In January 1980, after a long and painful fight against cancer, she died. Her death caused Castro much grief.

One other woman featured in Castro's life. Nati Revuelta, blonde and beautiful, had attended schools in France and the United States before becoming a student at Havana University. In 1952 she met Castro. She was a rich socialite. She played tennis at Vedado Tennis Club and enjoyed parties at the Biltmore Yacht Club. She married a wealthy physician but, with a social conscience, she showed revolutionary sympathies. She and Castro fell in love. It was the beginning of the end of both her and Castro's marriages, when she became Castro's mistress. She lent him the key of the Vedado mansion in Havana, where he was able to plot the path of his revolution. In addition, by pawning her valuable jewellery, she was able to finance his attack on the Moncada Barracks. In turn, he employed her to deliver both to politicians and to the press, the manifesto which he was proposing to issue after the attack on the Moncada barracks. When he was imprisoned after the attack, they wrote a large number of love letters to each other. They shared intellectual pursuits. They read the same books at the same time and exchanged views about them. They wrote about literature, philosophy and love. He wrote: "I want to share with you every pleasure I find in a book—Doesn't this mean that you are my intimate companion and that I am never alone." On another occasion he wrote: "I am on fire. Write to me, for I cannot be without your letters. I love you very much."

It did not take too long after the defeat of Batista for Castro to exercise his power. Leo Urritia, who had been elected President, accused Castro of being a communist and had frustrated Castro's attempts, as Prime Minister, to introduce social reform. On 17

July, Castro resigned as Prime Minister. He had had enough of the President, and on 19 July, he engineered his resignation. On 26 July, before an enormous crowd of supporters, he withdrew his own resignation and accepted the commands of the people. Thereafter he became known as the Maximum Leader. He immediately introduced a number of social reforms. Land was redistributed among the peasants. Improved education and health provisions were introduced. Separate facilities for blacks and whites were abolished. Public trials of those alleged under Batista to have committed murder and torture were held and some 600 were convicted and executed. Some were held in the Sports Palace, before an audience of fifteen thousand spectators, and the proceedings were carried live on radio and on television. When a trial of some forty members of Batista's Air Force were acquitted, Castro ordered a new trial which resulted in their convictions and sentences of long terms of imprisonment. Few of those charged at the trials were acquitted. The reaction of world opinion was universally hostile.

The United States had had a large financial interest in Cuba and had established profitable economic arrangements in exchange for support of the Batista regime. They naturally viewed the new regime with distrust. American property was nationalised. The Americans retaliated by withdrawing technicians necessary to run the Cuban economy and by reducing and eventually stopping their purchases of Cuban sugar. In March 1960, Eisenhower approved a CIA plan to invade Cuba and, when Kennedy became President, Kennedy decided to go ahead with the plan. It resulted in a disaster for the invaders at the Bay of Pigs. It was a public humiliation for the Americans and a huge propaganda victory for Castro. Because of American sanctions, Castro had turned more and more to the Soviet Union for economic and military aid. The arrival of Russian missiles in Cuba in September 1962 gave rise to a confrontation between Russia and America which threatened to escalate into a nuclear war.

The Cuban Missile crisis, as the event came to be known, ended with the Russians turning back their ships carrying missiles, and the Cubans agreeing to dismantle those in Cuba. In exchange, the Americans agreed that they would not invade Cuba and would deal with their bases in Turkey. For a while Castro was furious at what he saw as a betrayal by his Russian allies but, gradually, their relations improved. Visits by Castro to Russia, where he was greeted by large and enthusiastic crowds, and a warm welcome from the Politburo, helped to cement their friendship. It also had the effect of ensuring Russia support for the Cuban economy. Castro continued to meddle in the affairs in the Caribbean and South America. He found time to interest himself in some of the African countries, preaching the virtues of Marxism. Gradually, as the years passed, Castro sought to restore Cuba to something like its pre-revolution status by welcoming visitors from abroad. But, while the tourists flourished, the islanders saw no real increase in their standard of living. As Castro slipped into the background, sanctions have now finally been lifted while Castro's part in the history of Cuba will stand the test of time, as will the part played by his mistresses.

CHAPTER TWENTY THREE

JOHN F. KENNEDY AND AMERICAN PRESIDENTS

John Kennedy was the best known President to have had affairs with women whilst in office, but he was not the first, nor certainly the last. Thomas Jefferson was one of the Founding Fathers and one of the most distinguished Presidents. At his plantation at Montecello, there were a number of black slaves. One such was Sarah Hemmings, whom Jefferson had met in Paris and brought with him to America. Between them, they had five children and, in his will, he directed that Sarah and the children be freed from slavery. Warren Harding, who was President from 1921 until 1923, did not have the same reputation as a President. Although, when he died, he was apparently deeply mourned, he was subsequently ranked as the last among the 29 Presidents considered by a poll in1948.[302]

This was due to two particular criticisms: the first was that he ran an administration, some of whose members exercised their power corruptly; and, the second, that his extra marital love life was a matter of public scandal. The first political problem was known as the Veterans' Bureau scandal. This arose from a scheme to build hospitals for Veterans, organised by its director, Charles Forbes. There was no public consultation. Forbes engaged two construction firms privately and the three of them divided the profits of the venture between them. Forbes also sold valuable hospital supplies, stockpiled during the war, to an inside

---

302 Schlesinger. Arthur.M. (*Historians Rate the U.S Presidents*. Life Magazine. November.*1948*) pp 66-74

contractor. Before he could be charged with dishonesty, Harding allowed Forbes to escape to France where, after Harding's death, he returned to be tried in Chicago.

The next political scandal was known as the Teapot Dome. It involved an oil reserve in Wyoming. In 1921, it came under the jurisdiction of the Interior Secretary, Albert Fall. Leases were arranged by him without public scrutiny and he received substantial bribes for the granting of the leases. These were said to have had the approval of Harding. It was not until 1929 that Fall was convicted of corruption. Another scandal involved Harding's Attorney General, Harry Daugherty. He was twice tried for fraud but, although he refused to give evidence on his own behalf, a jury were twice unable to reach a verdict. Others of Harding's political appointees proved equally corrupt.

In 1891, Harding had married Florence Kling. They had no children. Harding was reputed to have had love affairs with two women. The first was with the wife of an Ohio department store owner, Camie Phillips, to whom Harding wrote some 250 love letters between 1909 and 1920.The affair lasted about fifteen years. She was according to one account: "the love of Harding's life –the enticements of his mind and body combined in one person."[303] When Harding was on course to be President, Phillips threatened to publish the story of the relationship, unless a substantial sum were paid to his wife. The Republican Party, fearful of the effect such a scandal would have on the prospects of their candidate being elected as President, paid Mrs Phillips a substantial lump sum and sent her and her family off to Japan. In addition she received a monthly sum. Harding's wife was well aware of the relationship and, although Harding was said to have died of a heart attack, some believe she poisoned him.

The other lady in his life was Nan Britton, who bore his child Elizabeth Ann, in 1919. She was his mistress all the time he was President. She wrote a sensational story of their affair, *The President's Daughter*, including the claim that they had sex in a

303 Russell, Francis. *The Shadow of Blooming Grove. Warren, G, Harding in his Times.*(Easton Press. Norwalk. CT. U.S.A. 1968) p 167

White House closet while Secret Service agents were close by to intercept intruders. She destroyed his correspondence but alleged that Harding had paid a monthly sum for the upkeep of his daughter. She died in 1991.

Franklin D. Roosevelt was President for an unprecedented three terms from 1933 until 1945. His marriage to Eleanor was not a very happy one and, when she discovered that he was having an affair with his social secretary, Lucy Mercer, she threatened to divorce him, unless he gave up Lucy. This he promised to do. He could not risk a scandal in his political life but, in fact, continued the affair for many years until his death, and Lucy Mercer was at his bedside when he died.

Dwight D. Eisenhower had been the successful Commander of the Allied forces in the invasion of North Africa and Europe during the Second World War. He was President from 1953 until 1961. He had, as his personal driver during the war, an English girl, Kate Summersby, with whom he started an affair while overseas. According to her autobiography, the love affair was never consummated, but there is serious doubt about her version of events. Eisenhower was married at the time to Mamie and when, during the war in 1945, he wanted to divorce her, he was not allowed to do so by General Marshall, then the Army Chief of Staff.

John Kennedy was always called Jack. He was the second son of Joseph Kennedy, a ruthless and highly ambitious politician who, having himself failed to become President, was determined that one of his sons should do so. Joseph, with an Irish background, had been the American Ambassador in London during the Second World War. He had enraged the British Government with his disparaging remarks about the ability of the British to fight, and with his obvious enthusiasm for the Hitler regime. In the result he was recalled to America in some disgrace and never achieved his ambition to be President. Jack served in the Navy during the war and was acclaimed as a hero, after his torpedo boat was sunk and he succeeded in rescuing some of the crew. His older brother was killed in the war and Joseph's political ambitions now rested on Jack. With his father's money and influence, Jack became a member of the House of Representatives for Massachusetts from 1947 to 1953. Thereafter, he was elected to the Senate, where he served until 1960. His period as a Senator was unremarkable but, in 1956, he was nominated as Vice-President by the Democratic National Convention. He lost to Senator Kefauver who, together with the Democratic nominee for president, Adlai Stevenson,were defeated by the Republicans in the 1956 election.

In 1960, Kennedy was elected President. It was a great personal triumph for the Kennedy family, overcoming what was then widely perceived as the difficult problem of Jack's Catholic faith. His inauguration speech was a remarkable call to his generation. In it he said: "Let the word go forth from this time and place to friend and foe alike, that the torch has been passed to a new generation of Americans, born in this century, tempered by war, disciplined by hard and bitter peace, part of our ancient heritage and, unwilling to witness or permit the slow undoing of those human rights to which the nation has always been committed and to which we are committed today, at home and around the world.—Let every nation know whether it wishes us well or ill, that we shall pay any price, bear any burden, meet any hardship, support any friend, oppose any foe, to secure the survival of success and liberty—And so, my fellow Americans, ask not what your country can do for you; ask what you can do for your country."

The nation was electrified. It appeared that a new dawn had arrived and that the fresh administration would introduce a significant and historic change in domestic and foreign policy. Sadly the glamour of the "New Frontier" never fulfilled the dream. Kennedy's period as President, revered by his admirers, has, with the passage of time, come to be regarded as one of non-fulfilment. His first venture into foreign politics was to allow an invasion of Cuba which, under the name the "Bay of Pigs", resulted in a humiliating defeat of the American backed venture. More successful, and certainly vastly more important, was his decision to deal with the Cuban Missile crisis in which, by delicate diplomacy and a naval quarantine, he defused the threat of a nuclear war with Soviet Russia. He managed to get the Russians to sign a modest Test Ban Treaty and the economy accelerated with GDP expanding. He adopted a sympathetic stance to the civil rights protest, but his untimely death in 1963 meant that many of his policies never came to fruition.

On 12 September 1953, Kennedy married Jacqueline Bouvier. She had been born in 1929, the daughter of wealthy parents and had one sister, Caroline Lee. They had a family estate in East Hampton and a house in New York. In 1940 her parents were divorced and Jacqueline spent her childhood with her mother in Mclean, Virginia and Newport, Rhode Island and with her father in New York and Long Island. She was brought up as a Catholic and, after leaving school in 1947, she went first to Vassar College, then to the University of Grenoble and the Sorbonne. She finally graduated at the George Washington University with a BA degree in French literature. She was fluent in French and Spanish and was able, during her husband's campaign for the presidency, to speak publicly in Italian and Polish. Apart from her wide interest in the arts, she was a dedicated horse woman. She was to give birth to a still born daughter, Arabella, in 1956 and in 1963 to Patrick who died two days later. The Kennedys had two other children, Caroline, born in November 1957 and John, born in November 1960. Kennedy suffered from a number of medical conditions. Apart from severe and chronic back pain, he was diagnosed with having Addison's disease, together with another endocrine disease. He was taking a basket of medication, as a result of which he appeared to suffer from hyperactivity, mood swings and an increase in virility. They may have been responsible for Kennedy's desire for extra-marital sex, best illustrated by the story that, during the course of a meeting with Harold Macmillan, he is alleged to have said: "I wonder how it is for you, Harold? If I don't get a woman for three days, I get terrible headaches."[304]

If all the rumours are to be believed, the number of women with whom he had sex ran into hundreds. Among those are

---

304 Reeves, Richard. *President Kennedy. Profile of Power.* (Simon & Schuster. New York 1993) p 290

Marilyn Monroe, Marlene Dietrich, Judith Campbell, Gunilla van Post, Mimi Alford, Mary Pichot Meyer, Angie Dickinson, Joan Lundberg, Pamela Tutnure, Alicia Purdom and many others. There were a whole group of starlets, call girls, prostitutes and staff members, who indulged Kennedy, sometimes in the White House, sometimes in the Georgetown house, in London and in Santa Monica. It was reported that, before his debates with Nixon, and on the eve of his inauguration, he had sex with call girls. The power was not only sexual. There is the story of his inviting Judith Campbell, his mistress, to his house in Georgetown while Jackie, now pregnant, was in Florida. Judith was having an affair with the head of the Chicago Mafia, Sam Giancana and Kennedy was anxious to meet him to secure his support in his election campaign. It paid off, because large sums of Mafia money were subsequently donated to the Kennedy campaign.

Kennedy is one of the best examples of the aphrodisiac of power. Undoubtedly he was a charming person in his own right, but the status of President enhanced his sexual appeal, which he was not slow to indulge. The exercise of the power to summon any girl that he wanted was irresistible, as was the power to ensure the silence of the girl by threats. Few girls would be able to reject the idea of sex with a President, more particularly if it were to occur in the White House or at his home. The vanity of the prey was thus an essential part of the successful exercise by the President of his power, as predator.

Lyndon Johnson was Kennedy's Vice-President, at the time of the latter's assassination in 1963, and was President until 1969. He had a number of affairs, the longest lasting being his affair with Madeline Brown. She had become pregnant in 1960 and gave birth to a son called Steven. The affair lasted some twenty years. Johnson's press secretary wrote in his biography of Johnson: "LBJ had the instincts of a Turkish Sultan in Istanbul."

Bill Clinton's affairs are second only in number to John Kennedy's. Many and varied were the women, the occasions and the venues. When Clinton was Governor of Arkansas, the State troopers reported affairs with dozens of girls. Some became household names. Gennifer Flowers and Sally Perdue were among them. When Clinton moved into the White House in 1993, nothing changed and his extramarital affairs continued. His relationship with Monica Lewinsky was a national scandal and gave rise to a proposal to impeach the President which was never pursued.

CHAPTER TWENTY FOUR

CONCLUSION

The exercise of power takes many forms and leads to many different results. Sometimes the results are far removed from the hope
and expectation of holder of the power. The Harmsworths are
a good example of this. Sometimes like Edward VIII and Mrs
Simpson or Reynaud and Comtesse Helene Portes, the prey is
transformed into the predator. One constant, however is the
foolish, reckless, excitement, involved for the predator and sometimes for the prey Oscar Wilde's description of "feeding with
panthers "was apt not only in his case but in others. As Parris
wrote "it involves danger secrecy and sometimes shame"[305]What
drove Asquith, when he was meant to be running a war, to spend
his time writing constantly to Venetia and wasting time and energy
reading and re reading her letters.? And did it never occur to
Gladstone that his interest in prostitutes might affect his political
career?

Allied to the excitement involved in illicit and illegal actions is
the extraordinary self-belief in powerful people that they create
their own good luck and that they can continue in their ways
until, no doubt, to their dismay "something big and external to
themselves finally fells them." Does this help to explain how
fraudsters like Bottomley and Maundy Gregory could continue
year after year to deceive the public into subscribing to their
blandishments. Owen described "the intoxication of power" as
a form of hubris which included "excessive confidence in their

---

305 Parris pxiii

own judgements."[306]The power to attract sexual favours is not limited to politicians or Royalty. People in public life, famous for being famous, have the same ability which they are not afraid to exploit but it is politicians who have attracted most comment, Parris was right to analyse their pathology –"elective office feeds your vanity and starves your self-respect."[307]

What was in it for the prey in an affair with a powerful man? For many like Lloyd George and Parnell the result was a happy relationship where the prey enjoyed equal satisfaction. But for the most part the prey were content to engage in an illicit affair, to share state secrets and to be consulted about important decisions. There was also the enormous prestige and glamour surrounding a relationship with a man of power in addition, sometimes, to the financial rewards involved. Thus predator and prey played their own individual part.

306 Owen pp1&2
307 Spectator 21 May 2011

SYNOPSIS

This book highlights how powerful people exercise that power. Politicians like Lloyd George and Gladstone, Kennedy and Clinton, Mussolini and Castro and Royalty like Edward VII and Edward VIII used it to attract women like butterflies to a flame. Sometimes they are newspaper magnates like the Harmsworths and Beaverbrook who tried dictating policy to Governments. Or con men like Bottomley and Maundy Gregory who used their power of persuasion to defraud greedy investors. Why do they do it? They all have an exaggerated self belief in their own importance. For the predator, power is indeed, the ultimate aphrodisiac

Lightning Source UK Ltd.
Milton Keynes UK
UKOW02n1426061016

284639UK00002B/33/P